BEHAVIORAL FINANCE

WHAT EVERYONE NEEDS TO KNOW®

BEHAVIORAL FINANCE

WHAT EVERYONE NEEDS TO KNOW®

H. KENT BAKER, GREG FILBECK, AND JOHN R. NOFSINGER

OXFORD
UNIVERSITY PRESS

OXFORD

UNIVERSITY PRESS

Oxford University Press is a department of the University of Oxford. It furthers the University's objective of excellence in research, scholarship, and education by publishing worldwide. Oxford is a registered trade mark of Oxford University Press in the UK and certain other countries.

"What Everyone Needs to Know" is a registered trademark of Oxford University Press.

Published in the United States of America by Oxford University Press 198 Madison Avenue, New York, NY 10016, United States of America.

Library of Congress Cataloging-in-Publication Data
Names: Baker, H. Kent (Harold Kent), 1944– author. | Filbeck, Greg, author. | Nofsinger, John R., author.
Title: Behavioral finance : what everyone needs to know® / H. Kent Baker, Greg Filbeck, John R. Nofsinger.
Description: New York, NY : Oxford University Press, [2019] | Includes index.
Identifiers: LCCN 2018019087 (print) | LCCN 2018020904 (ebook) |
ISBN 978–0–19–086875–8 (UPDF) | ISBN 978–0–19–086876–5 (EPUB) |
ISBN 978–0–19–086873–4 (pbk. : alk. paper) |
ISBN 978–0–19–086874–1 (hardcover : alk. paper)
Subjects: LCSH: Finance—Psychological aspects. | Investments—Psychological aspects. | Investments—Decision making.
Classification: LCC HG4515.15 (ebook) | LCC HG4515.15 .B339 2019 (print) |
DDC 332.601/9—dc23
LC record available at https://lccn.loc.gov/2018019087

1 3 5 7 9 8 6 4 2

Paperback printed by LSC Communications, United States of America
Hardback printed by Bridgeport National Bindery, Inc., United States of America

CONTENTS

2. Cognitive Biases   41

3. Emotional Biases and Social-Cultural Influences   77

4. Investor Behavior   99

5. Nudge: The Influence of Frame Dependence   127

6. Cognitive Ability   163

PREFACE

Who Are the Authors?

H. Kent Baker, CFA, CMA, is University Professor of Finance
at the Kogod School of Business, American University, where
he served as the Chair of the Department of Finance and Real
Estate and headed the Finance Center of Excellence. Before
joining the faculty at American University, he held both faculty and administrative positions at the business schools
of Georgetown University and the University of Maryland.
Professor Baker has consulting and training experience with
more than 100 organizations and is a former President of
the Southern Finance Association. He has published more
than 175 refereed journal articles and written or edited 32
books, including several on behavioral finance, among them
Behavioral Finance: Investors, Corporations, and Markets and
Financial Behavior: Players, Services, Products, and Markets. His
book *Investor Behavior: The Psychology of Financial Planning
and Investing* received the 2015 USA Best Book Award in the
Business: Personal Finance/Investing category. *Investment
Traps Exposed: Navigating Investor Mistakes and Behavioral Biases*
(2017) was the 2017 Book Excellence Award Winner in Personal
Finance and the Bronze Medalist, 2018 Axiom Business Book
Award in Personal Finance/Retirement Planning/Investing.
He has received numerous awards for research, teaching, and

service including the University Scholar/Teacher of the Year. Professor Baker has a BSBA (management) from Georgetown University; an MBA (finance), MEd (educational administration), and DBA (finance) from the University of Maryland; and an MS (quantitative methods), MA (training and career development), PhD (educational administration and organizational development), and PhD (counseling and student development) from American University. In his spare time, he is a professional musician who plays five instruments and has recorded and toured.

Greg Filbeck, CFA, FRM, CAIA, CIPM, PRM, holds the Samuel P. Black III Professor of Finance and Risk Management at Penn State Erie, the Behrend College and serves as Director of the Black School of Business. He previously served as Senior Vice President of Kaplan Schweser and held academic appointments at Miami University (Ohio) and the University of Toledo, where he also served as the Associate Director of the Center for Family Business. Professor Filbeck has authored or edited eight books and published more than 95 refereed academic journal articles. Professor Filbeck conducts consulting and training worldwide. He currently serves as President of the CFA Society Pittsburgh and was previously the President of the CFA Society Toledo and the Southern Finance Association. He received the Impact on Practice Award from the Black School of Business in 2015, the outstanding teaching award among iMBA faculty in 2010 and 2012, and the Penn State Behrend Regents award for Outstanding Researcher in 2011, and was the 2013 recipient of the Penn State Behrend Outstanding Outreach Award. He has a BS (engineering physics) from Murray State University and an MS in Applied Statistics from Penn State University and holds a DBA (finance) from the University of Kentucky. Filbeck is a Professionally Registered Parliamentarian, is a qualified administrator of the Myers-Briggs Type Indicator, and has 12 years of experience in radio broadcasting.

John R. Nofsinger is the William H. Seward Endowed Chair in International Finance at the College of Business and Public Policy, University of Alaska, Anchorage (UAA). Before joining the faculty at UAA in 2014, he was a professor at Washington State University and held the Nihoul Faculty Fellow from 2008 to 2013. He also held an assistant professor appointment at Marquette University. Professor Nofsinger has authored or coauthored 11 finance trade books, textbooks, and scholarly books. His books have been translated into 11 languages. His book *The Psychology of Investing* is in its sixth edition and is popular with investment advisors. As one of the world's leading experts in behavioral finance, Professor Nofsinger is a frequent speaker on this topic and others. He is also a prolific scholar who has published 64 articles in prestigious scholarly journals and practitioner journals. He is most widely known in the area of behavioral finance, but is also widely known for the topic of socially responsible finance. Professor Nofsinger is often quoted or appears in the financial media. He received a BS (electrical engineering) from Washington State University, an MBA from Chapman University, and a PhD (finance) from Washington State University. In his spare time, he competes in Ironman triathlons.

Why Did We Write This Book?

We are longtime friends and have worked together for years editing books and writing articles. We all completed doctoral programs in finance and learned the principles and paradigms of standard finance. For much of our adult lives, we have been fascinated by the psychology of investing and market behavior. After years of studying and researching how market participants and markets behave, we became increasingly aware of the limitations of standard finance. Although standard finance does a good job explaining how people and markets should behave based on a set of restrictive assumptions, it often fails to adequately explain how normal people and markets actually behave. Behavioral finance offers another perspective that complements the traditional finance view.

During its early years, behavioral finance identified both behavioral biases and a myriad of anomalies that contradicted accepted theoretical predictions. However, it often did an incomplete job of explaining how investors and others could deal with these anomalies or mitigate biases. Behavioral finance has been revolutionizing economics and finance at the highest levels. This is well illustrated by the world's most prestigious prize, the Nobel Memorial Prize in Economic Sciences, being awarded for behavioral topics in recent years, starting with Daniel Kahneman and Vernon L. Smith in 2002, Robert J. Shiller in 2013, and Richard Thaler in 2017. Because much of the behavioral finance research is difficult to grasp by people not directly involved in the topic, we took this opportunity to help them gain such an understanding. This book is our attempt to identify not only what everyone needs to know about behavioral finance but also what they want to know about this captivating subject. Of course, only readers of this book can determine whether we have accomplished this goal.

What Is the Book About?

Before the emergence of behavioral finance, standard finance was the reigning paradigm in academic finance. Although standard finance provides many useful insights, it offers an incomplete and unrealistic picture of actual, observed behavior. For example, standard finance assumes that people are rational and financial markets are efficient. *Market efficiency* refers to the degree to which stock prices and other securities prices reflect all available, relevant information. If financial markets are efficient, the world becomes a simple place. If people always act rationally, then security prices would fully reflect the available information and investors would be unable to consistently beat the market. If this situation were true, the vast resources devoted to analyzing, selecting, and trading securities would be a waste of time and effort.

Yet, during the past several decades, substantial research evidence has shown that people are far less rational in their decision-making than initially assumed. Casual observation also supports this fact. Just ask yourself, "Do I always behave rationally when making economic or financial decisions?" If you are being honest, the answer is no. Further, such irrational behaviors are neither random nor senseless but instead are systematic and predictable. People often repeat the same cognitive mistakes because of how their brains work. Emotions and social-cultural influences also affect behavior. For example, the human brain often processes information using shortcuts and emotional filters that influence financial decision-makers in a seemingly irrational manner. Such behavior is pervasive in investor decisions, financial markets, corporate managerial behavior, and elsewhere. The impact of these suboptimal financial decisions has ramifications for personal wealth, the quality of life, and market efficiency. For example, evidence supporting a myriad of anomalies challenges many of the tenets of standard finance. An *anomaly* is evidence of behavior that contradicts an accepted theoretical prediction.

Given that everyone makes systematic mistakes in their decision-making processes, why not develop new strategies, tools, methods, and policies to help make better judgments and improve overall well-being? This objective is where behavioral finance enters the picture. The intent of behavioral finance is not to explain rational or irrational behavior, but to explain "normal" behavior. Behavioral finance offers an alternative view of behavior and financial markets that complements standard finance. As Dan Ariely noted in his book, *Predictably Irrational: The Hidden Forces That Shape Our Decisions*, "Wouldn't economics make a lot more sense if it were based on how people actually behave, instead of how they should behave?" Given both the breadth and depth of behavioral finance, the intent of this book is not to be all encompassing.

Trying to do everything for everyone is likely to be unproductive. Instead, the book's scope is more narrowly focused. Its main purpose is to discuss how behavioral finance primarily affects individuals, especially investors, not corporate managers, institutional investors, or policymakers. However, it also notes that behavioral finance offers evidence that appears anomalous from the efficient markets perspective and offers new predictions. This focus is justified given the considerable amount of evidence that documents the biases and associated problems with individual investor trading and portfolio allocations. The book's focus should be particularly appealing to those interested in learning how behavioral finance can help to explain their behavior and improve their financial decision-making.

Behavioral Finance: What Everyone Needs to Know offers a balanced explanation of the broad issues associated with behavioral finance in a succinct but authoritative manner. It follows a straightforward question-and-answer format that should be understandable to a diverse audience. The book is organized into six chapters, each containing questions relating to each chapter's focus. The format enables browsing for topics of interest without reading the book from cover to cover.

Whom Do We Want to Thank?

Not surprisingly, many people played important roles in bringing this book from the conceptual stage to final publication. Of course, the many researchers and writers who provided insights about behavioral finance over the past four decades serve as the foundation of this book. The reviewers of our initial book proposal offered valuable comments about the most important topics to include. Our partners at Oxford University Press performed at a highly professional level throughout the entire process. Dave Pervin (Senior Editor) offered detailed comments on our draft, suggested how to frame our presentation, and nudged us in that direction. Hayley Singer (Editorial

Assistant) did an admirable job in paying close attention to the many details necessary in moving the book along. Special thanks also go to Rajakumari Ganessin (Project Manager), Richard Isomaki (Copyeditor), Leslie Johnson (Production Editor), and Claudie Peterfreund (Indexer). Linda Baker merits special thanks for proofing the entire manuscript. We also recognize the support provided to us by our respective institutions: the Kogod School of Business at American University; the Black School of Business at Penn State Behrend; and the College of Business and Public Policy at the University of Alaska, Anchorage. Finally, we thank our families, to whom this book is dedicated: Linda and Rory Baker; Janis, Aaron, Andrea, Kyle, and Grant Filbeck; and Anna Nofsinger.

BEHAVIORAL FINANCE

WHAT EVERYONE NEEDS TO KNOW®

1

FOUNDATIONS AND PSYCHOLOGICAL CONCEPTS

Historically, those traveling the financial highway were taught to follow a single route. Travelers were told that as long as everyone faithfully followed directions and weather conditions were ideal, the road would be their best choice and they would get to their intended destination. Over time, however, some became disenchanted with the journey because the highway provided a bumpy ride due to ruts in the road and often failed to get them where they really wanted to go. Some adventuresome pioneers decided to bypass the old road and to build a new one. Although they initially encountered obstacles and resistance in forging a new path, they persisted in their endeavor and eventually attracted others to help them pave the way. These pioneers, called behaviorists, created a fork in the financial highway. As Yogi Berra, the famous baseball player and coach once said: "When you arrive at a fork in the road, take it." Unfortunately, strong commitment to existing paths and paradigms can obscure one's vision of promising alternatives.[1] A *paradigm* is a standard, perspective, or set of ideas. That is, a paradigm is a model or a way of looking at something. Not surprisingly, finance traditionalists were anxious about the entrance of behaviorists into the financial highway. Although many still travel the old road, the new road has attracted numerous travelers by offering an appealing choice with very different scenery along the way.

This simple story sets the stage for two major branches in finance: the well-established standard finance and the more recent behavioral finance. Standard finance rests on classical decision theory and presumes that individuals, institutions, and markets are rational. On average, these individuals are unbiased and maximize their own self-interests. Any errors that market participants make are uncorrelated and thus are unable to affect market prices. This approach assumes that people have internally consistent preferences, access to perfect information, can apply unlimited processing power to any available information, and make optimal choices by using expected utility theory to maximize the benefit they receive from an action, subject to constraints. This book does not focus on standard finance. Instead, it discusses the foundations of the new financial highway called behavioral finance.

What Is Behavioral Finance?

Behavioral finance is a relatively new and expanding field that has exploded in popularity, especially since the 1980s. It is not only interesting but also provides important insights into human and market behavior. The precise definition of behavioral finance is still debated, partly because this discipline is constantly evolving. For the purposes of this book, *behavioral finance* is the study of the influence of psychology and other disciplines on the behavior of financial practitioners and the subsequent effect on markets.[2] Additionally, behavioral finance focuses on applying psychological and economic principles for the improvement of financial decision-making.[3]

Although initially criticized by advocates of standard finance for encroaching on their territory, behavioral finance has become part of mainstream finance for the media, investment industry, and academics. In fact, several researchers in behavioral finance and experimental economics have received the Nobel Memorial Prize in Economic Sciences, including Daniel

Kahneman and Vernon L. Smith in 2002, Robert J. Shiller in 2013, and Richard Thaler in 2017. Behavioral finance tries to explain how people make economic decisions by combining behavioral and cognitive psychological theory with conventional finance and economic theory. In fact, behavioral finance is exhibited each time a person makes a financial decision. Research on behavioral biases—cognitive, emotional, and social-cultural—helps to explain errors in economic decision-making and to predict the behavior, especially the mistakes, of others, thus enabling them to guard against making similar errors in the future. However, the term "behavioral bias" must be used with caution because some behavioral biases can have positive outcomes.

Behavioral finance has evolved dramatically from what some considered a "pop science" and a collection of anomalies and biases to an explanation of financial phenomena. In a noninvesting context, an *anomaly* is a strange or unusual occurrence. Thus, anomalous behavior contradicts an accepted prediction or deviates from the common rule. In a behavioral context, *market anomalies* refer to situations when a security or group of securities performs contrary to the notion of efficient markets. As a result, they provide evidence that a given assumption or model does not hold in practice. Although some market anomalies are transient relations that disappear, others occur repeatedly. Theoretically, market anomalies should neither occur nor persist, but some do.

The cross-disciplinary nature of behavioral finance helps to clarify why people make the money choices they do, not dictate how they should make those choices. Behavioral finance has also revolutionized the way people think about what makes humans "tick" concerning money and why and how markets might be inefficient. However, this field of study is just beginning to understand the influences of human behavior as applied to individuals, firms, groups, or institutions making financial decisions.

Why Is Behavioral Finance Important to Practitioners?

Practitioners such as investors, financial planners and advisors, portfolio managers, corporate executives, among others, need to understand behavioral finance for several reasons. First, behavioral finance helps to explain various phenomena involving money and markets and to solve persistent problems and limitations previously addressed with the concepts of standard finance and classical economics. Evidence involving individual behavior often does not coincide with the predictions of traditional theories. However, the existence of anomalous evidence does not constitute proof that existing paradigms are necessarily "wrong." Behavioral finance offers a new set of explanations of anomalies and empirical regularities. According to Brooke Harrington, a noted financial researcher, "Learning about common cognitive errors in economic decision-making . . . feels like getting a peek inside the flawed machines that are our brains, making it seem possible to predict the behavior (particularly the mistakes) of others, and guard against them in oneself. In short, behavioral finance seems to offer insight and a sense of control, imposing order on what otherwise appears chaotic and unpredictable."[4]

Second, behavioral finance provides insights that help overcome the constraints of many traditional theories and models that rest on the belief that market participants act in a rational wealth-maximizing manner. Making this assumption severely limits the ability to make accurate or detailed predictions. Although normative models provide a basis for understanding some "idealized events," they fail to explain certain real-world events where people apparently behave irrationally and unpredictably. In other words, theoretical models try to simplify complicated things, but often do a poor job of explaining a messy real world inhabited by humans. Behavioral finance tries to fill the void between theory and practice by combining scientific insights into cognitive reasoning with conventional economic and financial theory. Behavioral finance provides a new body of theories and a new set of predictions that help to explain financial behavior and real-world markets. In doing so, it complicates the study of finance because the focus now turns to how people actually behave as opposed to how they should behave.

Third, behavioral finance is not a replacement of standard finance. Instead, it is a companion that complements standard finance. Given the complexities associated with decision-making, neither approach independently provides a comprehensive account in interpreting choice behavior. Both traditional and behavioral research in finance can identify many predictive successes and failures in their own areas. Thus, applying alternative approaches is likely to provide a more robust explanation of complex decision-making behavior than using a single viewpoint. However, given the evidence that has emerged over the past several decades, the time may be ripe to discard or at least substantially modify some of the established paradigms of standard finance

Fourth, behavioral finance studies have identified different behavioral biases that cause some people to behave irrationally and sometimes against their best interests. Although some behavioral biases are useful, most can lead to making costly mistakes. Behavioral finance provides a means of helping practitioners recognize their mistakes and those of others, comprehend the reasons for making these mistakes, and deal with them. Being knowledgeable about behavioral finance can help people avoid emotion-driven speculation leading to losses, and thus devise an appropriate wealth management strategy. At a collective or market level, understanding biases provides a clearer explanation of the severe rise and fall in asset prices that result in bubbles and crashes. Practitioners have a vested interest in learning about behavioral finance to make them more aware of their own decision-making processes.

What Are Some Cornerstones Underlying Behavioral Finance?

Behavioral finance theory rests on several assumptions, foundations, or characteristics. A major cornerstone of behavioral finance involves *investor sentiment*, which is a theory about how real-world investors actually form their beliefs and valuations. According to behavioral finance, people exhibit behavioral preferences, and information-processing biases preventing them from making the optimal choice. Hence, they are sometimes irrational or quasi-rational, a condition that is known as bounded rationality. *Bounded rationality* in decision-making occurs when the rationality of individuals is limited by the information they have, cognitive limitations of the human mind, and the finite amount of time they have to make decisions. Based on this view, decision-makers are *satisficers* who seek a satisfactory solution rather than an optimal one.[5]

Another assumption underlying behavioral finance is that individual errors and biases in processing information are correlated among other investors (systematic), so they don't average out at the market level. That is, even if the market contains individual biases, they don't cancel each other out to make the market, on aggregate, unbiased. This situation creates the possibility that correlated errors of investors could potentially last for long periods and affect prices accordingly, hence making markets inefficient.

In an *efficient market*, security prices reflect all available information at any point in time. In an *inefficient market*, securities such as common stocks are not always accurately priced and tend to deviate from their true or intrinsic value. Given the structure of markets, they are unlikely to be perfectly efficient, as clearly evidenced by recent asset bubbles. Although history reveals many asset bubbles, bubble production seems to have accelerated sharply. Thus, markets are not only inefficient, but also appear to be showing greater inefficiency than in the past.[6]

A cornerstone underlying behavioral finance involves limits to arbitrage in financial markets. *Arbitrage* involves a costless investment that generates riskless profits by taking advantage of mispricings across different instruments or markets representing the same security. Consider the following simple example of arbitrage. Company A's stock is trading for $50 on the New York Stock Exchange (NYSE) but for $50.10 on the London Stock Exchange (LSE). By buying the stock on the NYSE and immediately selling it on the LSE, a trader would earn a $0.10 profit per share, assuming no transaction or other costs. The trader could continue to take advantage of this arbitrage opportunity until the specialists on the NYSE exhaust their inventory of Company A's stock, or until the specialists on either exchange adjust their prices to eliminate this opportunity.

Arbitrage is critical in maintaining efficient markets because the arbitrage process keeps true values aligned with market prices. In practice, arbitrage entails both costs and the assumption of risk. Thus, limits exist to the effectiveness of arbitrage in eliminating certain security mispricings. *Limits to arbitrage* is a theory stating that prices remain in a nonequilibrium state for extended periods because of restrictions placed on funds that limit the ability of rational traders to arbitrage away the pricing inefficiencies.[7] Hence, limits to arbitrage could prevent rational investors from correcting price deviations caused by irrational investors. But in real-world financial markets, arbitrage is not close to being perfect.

Within behavioral finance, the information structure and the characteristics of market participants systematically are assumed to influence both individual decisions and market outcomes. Thus, investors aren't always rational, and markets can be inefficient.

What Is Prospect Theory and What Implications Does It Have for Choice Behavior?

Prospect theory describes how people make choices between different options or prospects that involve risk and uncertainty. Risk and uncertainty differ. *Risk* involves the ability to predict the different possibilities of a future outcome, while *uncertainty* does not. Thus, risk can be measured and quantified, but uncertainty can't. Daniel Kahneman and Amos Tversky, whom many view as the fathers of behavioral finance, created this theory in 1979 and later refined this descriptive model to reflect real-life choices, not optimal decisions, as normative models do.[8] They called it prospect theory because it is a catchy, attention-getting name. Thus, prospect theory provides an alternative to conventional wisdom as represented by expected utility theory and shows how people decide between alternatives that involve risk and uncertainty.[9] In 2002, Kahneman received the Nobel Prize for having integrated insights from psychological research into the economic sciences.

Expected utility theory provides the basis for much of standard finance theory. *Expected utility theory* involves analyzing situations where people must make a decision without knowing which outcomes may result from that decision. Hence, they are making decisions under uncertainty. According to expected utility theory, a person should choose the act resulting in the highest expected utility. *Utility* is the economist's term for satisfaction. The utility, or satisfaction, of each outcome is weighted according to the probability that the act will lead to that outcome. Evidence suggests that expected utility theory makes faulty predictions about people's decisions in many real-life choice situations. For example, expected utility theory asserts that no sane individual would play the lottery or gamble with poor odds. Yet lotteries and gambling are widespread.

Prospect theory provides the most widely accepted alternative to expected utility theory. In prospect theory, the value function has three important properties distinguishing it from the expected utility function. First, prospect theory measures value in terms of changes in wealth from a reference point, whereas a utility function measures value based on the level of final wealth. Thus, people are more concerned with changes to wealth than their long-run state of wealth. For this reason, many of the super wealthy aren't satisfied with having billions of dollars because they value how much their wealth increases more than the actual level.

Second, the value function is convex when facing losses, which reflects risk-taking to avoid loses. But the function is concave for gains, which reflects risk aversion. An individual's utility function evaluates satisfaction from the perspective of risk aversion, risk neutrality, or risk attraction. Thus, investors are both risk-seekers and risk-averters at the same time. In economics and finance, a *risk-seeker* or *risk-lover* is a person who has a preference for risk, such as casino-goers. Such individuals search for greater volatility and uncertainty in investments in exchange for anticipated higher returns. Most investors are considered *risk-averse*, meaning they prefer lower returns with known risks rather than higher returns with unknown risks. In other words, risk averse investors facing two investments with the same expected return but different risks would prefer the alternative with the lower risk.

Third, prospect theory recognizes the asymmetry of human choices. People attach greater weight to losses than to equivalent gains in wealth. That is, losses are more painful in magnitude than a similar profit is pleasurable. *Loss aversion* refers to the tendency to prefer avoiding a loss to taking a chance on receiving an equivalent gain. People often choose to minimize losses because losses have a greater impact on their psyche than gains, even with the probability of those losses being small. Thus, loss aversion implies that the pain from a $1,000 loss is greater than the pleasure from a $1,000 gain. Kahneman and Tversky were the first to show that people experience almost twice as much pain from a loss compared to the pleasure of a similar-sized gain. Loss aversion is a problem when it leads people to go to irrational lengths to avoid taking risks. Under expected utility theory, individuals don't attach a differential weight to losses or gains.[10]

Let's look at several examples to illustrate various implications of prospect theory for choice behavior.[11] People tend to have greater interest in their relative gains and losses than in their final income and wealth. But relative gains and losses require a *reference point* or anchor, which is a point used to find or describe the location of something. According to prospect theory, the reference point determines how an outcome is perceived. The reference point is often the prior level of wealth, but it could also be the wealth of someone you know. If your relative position does not improve, then you are unlikely to feel better off, despite having an increase in wealth. For example, assume that two investors know one another. If both investor A and investor B receive a 10% return on their portfolios, neither will feel better off. However, if investor A receives a 10% return on his portfolio and investor B gets a 0% return, investor A feels much wealthier regardless of the level of his wealth.

Here is another example. According to prospect theory, people tend to be loss-averse and give greater weight to losses than to gains. To illustrate: an investor who gains $1,000 on one stock and loses $750 on another may consider this situation a net loss in terms of satisfaction, despite coming out $250 ahead. Prospect theory also explains why individuals might sell assets of increasing value (winners) too soon to secure gains and hold losing assets (losers) for too long, hoping that the value of these assets will increase. Losses cause more severe pain than the pleasure resulting from a gain of the same magnitude.

As a final example, people strongly prefer certainty and will sacrifice returns to achieve greater certainty. For instance, assume you have two options: (1) a guaranteed win of $1,000 and (2) a 75% chance of winning $1,500 but a 25% chance of winning nothing. You are apt to select the first option with a sure gain of $1,000, even though the second has a higher expected gain, computed as $[0.75(\$1,500) + 0.25(\$0)] = \$1,125$.

What Is the Disposition Effect and Why Is It Harmful to Investors?

Does the saying "Cut your losses and let your profits run" sound familiar? Although this common investment advice is intended to help people engage in disciplined investment management, many investors have difficulty following it. The *disposition effect* is a tendency to realize gains quickly and defer the realization of losses. This term is shorthand for the pre-disposition toward "get-evenitis," which is the tendency for investors to hold on to a losing investment until its price returns to the original amount at which they bought the asset.[12] People exhibit this bias when they say, "If the price would just go back to what I paid, I would sell it." Of course, that is not a convincing argument for owning that stock. Empirical studies conducted with stocks and other assets such as real estate show strong support for the disposition effect.[13] However, conflicting evidence suggests that in panics, people often sell stocks that are falling in price too quickly, thus precipitating market crashes.

Although a full understanding of the underlying causes of the disposition effect is currently lacking, especially based on rational explanations, investor psychology appears to play an important role. One explanation involves *self-justification*, which describes how, when someone encounters a situation in which that person's behavior is inconsistent with his beliefs, that person has a tendency to justify the behavior and deny any negative feedback associated with the behavior. People often have difficulty accepting and admitting their own mistakes because doing so is unpleasant and sometimes painful. Investors hate losses and are willing to gamble to avoid experiencing them, so they exhibit risk-seeking behavior by holding losers.

Another behavioral reason for the disposition effect is that investors may lack the self-control to sell a losing investment. *Self-control* refers to the ability to regulate one's emotions, thoughts, and behavior when facing temptations and impulses. Hence, investors may hold on to losing investments, hoping these investments will eventually return to their initial purchase prices. Selling the loser makes the regret of buying it in the first place feel stronger. Yet investors want to lock in gains because doing so demonstrates that they made good investment decisions. That is, selling winners evokes the pleasant feeling of pride. Consequently, investors exhibit risk-averse behavior by selling winners. Thus, investors avoid regret and seek pride. A third explanation for the disposition effect involves prospect theory, but the evidence shows mixed results.[14]

The disposition effect is harmful to investors for several reasons. First, suffering from the disposition effect can be detrimental to investors' performance and increase the chances of making bad decisions. Selling winners too soon and holding on to losers too long increases the capital gains taxes that investors pay and reduces returns even before taxes. A *capital gains tax* is a tax levied on profits an investor realizes when selling a capital asset, such as a stock, for a price that is higher than the purchase price. Investors often realize gains on their investments but don't take offsetting losses. As a result, they pay higher taxes because capital gains are based on realized gains, not on overall portfolio returns. Additionally, the stocks that investors sell (the winners) as a result of the disposition effect often outperform those that they hold (the losers). So they are holding the wrong stocks. Thus, investors need to regulate their behavior to achieve specific goals.

Second, the disposition effect can affect rational decision-making. The historical price that an investor paid for an asset such as a stock is irrelevant to decision-making because it represents a *sunk cost*, which is a cost that has already been incurred and can't be recovered. Investors should not "cry over spilled milk" because they can't undo something that has already taken place. The decision to sell or hold a security should depend on its perceived future value, not the initial purchase price. Yet investors often use the initial price as a reference point for interpreting investment performance.

Generally speaking, investors would be better off holding well-performing stocks longer and selling losing stocks sooner. Investors who engage in *momentum investing* try to capitalize on the continuance of existing trends in the market. The general idea underlying momentum investing is that once a trend is established, it is more likely to continue in that direction than to move against the trend. By holding winners longer, investors may experience momentum in which winning stocks continue to rise in price. By selling a security that has been in a downtrend sooner, investors may realize a higher price than waiting until later to sell. Academic research provides support for momentum investing.[15]

To counter the disposition effect, investors can place a stop-loss order in the market. A *stop-loss order* is an order to sell a security or commodity at a specified price in order to limit a loss. Other strategies that investors use to sell losers are to group all of the loser stocks in the portfolio and sell them all at once to "get it over with." Also, investors sometimes sell a winner and a loser together to reduce the pain of regret for the loser. Interestingly, people tend to spread out the selling of winners over time to prolong the feeling of pride.[16]

What Are Heuristics?

Have you ever made a decision based on an educated guess, rule of thumb, or common sense? If so, you have used a heuristic. Heuristics are a key theme in behavioral finance. *Heuristic* are simple, efficient rules that people frequently use to help increase the speed of making decisions and forming judgments. Strategies that provide shortcuts to problem-solving and decisions take one's personal experience into account. By using heuristics, the brain generates estimates before fully digesting the available information. This process, called *heuristic simplification*, generally gets people where they want to go but sometimes sends them off course when considering investment decisions.[17]

Within behavioral finance, heuristics relate to making financial decisions in a fast and frugal manner. *Fast and frugal heuristics* refer to simple, task-specific decision strategies that are part of a decision-maker's repertoire of cognitive strategies for solving judgment and decision tasks.[18] Decision-makers often face a set of choices with uncertainty and a limited ability to quantify the likelihood of the results. Heuristics represent mental shortcuts that enable them to focus on one aspect of a complex problem and ignore others. Consequently, by using simple rules, people can make decisions more quickly and efficiently. This practical approach to processing data does not guarantee an optimal or perfect result, but it often provides one sufficient to meet the immediate goals.

Uncertainty plays an important role in adopting heuristics. For example, investors often lack sufficient information about the future trends in security prices, so they adopt ad hoc rules to make investment decisions. Although heuristics are helpful in many situations, they can also result in poor outcomes and bad decisions. Behavioral finance recognizes that people who rely on heuristics make errors, but standard finance does not. Standard finance assumes that people make perfectly rational decisions, apply unlimited processing power to any available information, and can assign probabilities to each potential outcome. They then correctly apply the appropriate tools to reach an optimal outcome. By contrast, behavioral finance makes none of these assumptions because they are unrealistic in practice. Thus, a heuristics and biases framework serves as a counterpart to standard finance theory's asset-pricing models.

Let's examine a couple of examples using heuristics—one in everyday life and another in investments. The everyday life example involves the *authority heuristic*, which occurs when someone believes the opinion of a person on a subject just because the individual is an authority figure. The strength of the bias to obey a legitimate authority figure is a result of systemic socialization practices intended to instill in people the perception that such obedience represents correct behavior. People often apply this heuristic in matters such as science, education, and hierarchical organizations such as the military. For instance, when a scientist confirms a specific finding, laymen are likely to accept this judgment because an authority figure's statement sounds convincing. Students often believe a professor's opinion because such individuals usually possess higher degrees of knowledge on the topic.

Another example of a popular heuristic used in investing concerns buying mutual funds. Given the large number of mutual funds available, investors face a potentially complex task of deciding which fund to buy. To facilitate this process, they may decide to choose funds by extrapolating past performance into the future. For example, consider the following simple rule: Past performance is the best indicator of future performance, so select funds with the highest Morningstar ratings. The *Morningstar risk rating* is a ranking given to publicly traded mutual funds and exchange-traded funds (ETFs) by the investment research firm Morningstar. The ratings range from one to five stars: one being the poorest rank and five being the best. The problem with this heuristic is that yesterday's big winners could become tomorrow's big losers. Using past risk-adjusted performance to guide investment decisions might work in very short time periods, but there is little consistency in predictive ability beyond this short-term horizon. That is, top-performing funds typically don't continue to significantly outperform other funds over long periods.[19] Although momentum investing has potential merits if properly executed, it also involves risks.[20] Hence, buying "past winners" is a tempting but flawed investing strategy over the long term.

What Role Do Heuristics Play in Forming Judgments and Making Decisions?

People use heuristics to form judgments and make decisions for several reasons. First, they employ heuristics because their brains have a natural need for closure. Thinking is hard work. The brain uses different strategies to process information, make judgments, and solve problems. Some approaches are complex and others are quick. To decrease the amount and complexity of information requiring analysis, the brain excludes some information and uses shortcuts to simplify the process. In some instances, heuristics can actually be beneficial by enabling quicker judgments, thus reducing the time and mental effort spent researching and analyzing information to solve a problem and to control for extreme complexity. These mental processes are particularly appropriate for decision-making under uncertainly.

Second, heuristics help to avoid *paralysis by analysis*, which is the state of overanalyzing or overthinking a situation so that a decision or action is never taken, in effect paralyzing the outcome. Consider a paradox in philosophy called "Buridan's ass" that involves the concept of free will. In this hypothetical situation, a hungry donkey is placed between two bales of hay that are exactly the same distance from the donkey. Which bale of hay will the donkey choose to eat? According to the paradox, the donkey can't make any rational decision because the bales are equidistant. Thus, the donkey starves to death because of its paralysis.

Although heuristics can sometimes be helpful by saving time, effort, and energy, they often are instinctive and irrational. Using heuristics can hinder the development of new ideas and lead to systematic and predictable mistakes, causing intelligent people to make poor decisions, such as when investing. As Hersh Shefrin, who is one the first financial economists to incorporate ideas from psychologists into working theories, notes, "Because of their reliance on heuristics, practitioners hold biased beliefs that render them vulnerable to committing errors."[21]

Four general categories or types of general purpose heuristics are representativeness, availability, anchoring, and affect. The first three heuristics can lead to psychological biases and systematic errors in how people think, while the fourth relates to emotions, or how people feel. What follows is a discussion of each of these types of heuristics.

How Does the Representativeness Heuristic Influence Judgment and Decision-Making Behavior?

Let's examine a classic example by Amos Tversky and Daniel Kahneman that illustrates how the representativeness heuristic can influence perceptions of other people.[22] Assume that you perceive someone as shy and withdrawn, with little interest in people or in the world of reality. This person is tidy and meek and has a need for order and structure, as well as a passion for detail. Which of the following professions is this individual likely to practice: farmer, salesman, airline pilot, librarian, or physician? Based on the representativeness heuristic and stereotypes about these professions, you probably thought that this person was a librarian. This snap judgment about someone's occupation based on knowing about a few personality traits is likely to result in a hasty and erroneous conclusion. However, if you assessed the accuracy of at least some of the reported traits, you might have drawn a different conclusion.

The *representativeness heuristic*, also called *representative bias*, is the tendency to use past experiences or beliefs to guide the decision-making process.[23] In making quick judgments, people often compare a person, event, or object to a prototype or representative idea that already exists in their mind that they tend to view as similar or dissimilar based on how it matches up with their model. Although this heuristic is useful in making judgments quickly, it can also lead to poor choices, stereotypes, and errors because people often have a skewed belief about the past. Why? Representativeness presumes that once people or events are categorized, they share all the features of other members in that category, which plays into stereotypes of people and events. Another downside of using the representativeness heuristic is the tendency to ignore other courses of action besides the one that immediately springs to mind.

Here are two examples of representativeness in investments. Investors may prefer to buy a stock that has had abnormally high recent returns (the *extrapolation bias*) or may misconstrue a company's positive characteristics, such as producing high-quality goods, as an indicator of a good investment.[24] Let's examine the extrapolation bias a bit more. One example is when investors might be tempted to forecast a company's future earnings based on a short history of past high earnings. However, this form of stereotyping can lead to overestimating or underestimating a company's future performance because past earnings may be an inappropriate guideline for its future. Although every prospectus points out that past performance does not guarantee future results, investors often ignore this warning. A *prospectus* is a formal legal document that is required by and filed with the Securities and Exchange Commission (SEC) that provides details about an investment offered for sale to the public. Unfortunately, investors may fail to take into account that the high earnings could result from chance and be unlikely to reoccur. Or the stock's price might have already adjusted to the growth rate and thus may not be a good investment going forward. Another example is that, during the early phase of a stock market or housing bubble, market participants erroneously conclude that prices will continue to rise into the future. Similarly, when prices have been falling, investors have mental difficulty getting back into the market because this bias leads them to believe that prices will continue to fall.

If you are prone to representative bias, you can begin to lessen this tendency by being aware of the likelihood of a particular event based on situational information. You should look for ways to introduce objectivity into the decision-making process. You can also surround yourself with people who challenge your opinions and listen carefully and empathetically to your views.

What Are Two Common Biases Associated with the Representative Heuristic?

Two common biases associated with the representativeness heuristic relate to the law of small numbers and mean reversion. The *law of small numbers* is a fallacy in which people assume that a small sample is representative of a much larger population. As a result of not considering the sample size, people often derive rules from small groups that are reliable only in much larger sample sizes.

A classic example is a coin toss. If tossing a coin results in heads, say, seven times in a row, the inclination is to predict an increase in the likelihood that the next coin toss will be tails, "evening things out." Given that the probability of a fair coin being heads or tails is 50% each time the coin is flipped, the percentages should balance out. Right? This belief is incorrect in the short run. Those probabilities can be quite skewed in small samples because each toss is an independent event unconnected to the toss before or after it.

The bias in this example, called the *gambler's fallacy*, is the belief that past events influence the future even when each event is unrelated to the previous one. This fallacy is a glitch in thinking. Those committing the gambler's fallacy expect past events to influence the probability of something happening in a game of chance. Thus, if gamblers playing games that draw numbers, such as keno, roulette, and a lottery, believe that a number is "due" because it has not been drawn lately, they would be surprised to be told that the odds have not changed.

Now let's apply the gambler's fallacy to an investment example. Assume that the Standard & Poor's 500 Index (S&P 500) has closed higher 10 trading sessions in a row. The *S&P 500* is an index of 500 stocks seen as a leading indicator of U.S. equities and is widely regarded as the best single gauge of the performance of large-cap U.S. equities. *Market capitalization (cap)* refers to the number of shares outstanding times the share price. If you believe that after 10 up days the odds of a market decline are higher, you could enter into a short sale on the SPDR S&P 500 exchange-traded fund (ETF). Before proceeding, let's explain each of these terms. *Short selling* is the sale of a security that is not owned by the seller. The short seller borrows the stock from a broker and then sells it at the current market price, with the sale proceeds credited to the short seller's margin account. The seller is motivated to enter a short sale based on the belief that a security's price will decline, enabling the seller to buy it back at a lower price to make a profit. *SPDR* is an acronym for the Standard & Poor's Depositary Receipts, now the SPDR S&P 500. An *ETF* is a type of investment fund that is traded on a stock exchange. This ETF is designed to track the S&P 500 stock market index. On a purely statistical basis, past events don't connect to future events. Although various reasons could explain a market downturn on the eleventh day, the fact that the market was up 10 days in a row is irrelevant. Although many people likely believed that increasing nine days in a row would result in a down day on the tenth day, the market actually went up that day. As previously mentioned, investors should be aware that past performance is no guarantee of future results.

Another bias associated with representativeness is the failure to allow for *mean reversion* or *regression toward the mean*, which is the reversion of outcomes toward computed averages over long periods of time. Investors often ignore the fact that extreme performance usually returns to the average. Thus, both high-performing and low-performing mutual funds— winners and losers—tend to revert to the averages over time.

An implication of such biases is that market participants are inclined to over- or underestimate the performance of stocks or mutual funds that have achieved results either above or below the market average in recent years. Stocks with better performance than the market for several years often subsequently have results that are worse than the averages. Underperforming stocks in the past often outperform in the future.

What Is the Availability Heuristic and How Can It Affect Investment Decisions?

Certain events are likely to stand out in your mind more than others. For example, after hearing a highly publicized news report about big lottery winners, you start to overestimate your likelihood of winning the lottery. Consequently, you increase your spending on lottery tickets. This real-life example illustrates the availability heuristic in which related events or situations immediately spring to mind when you are trying to make a decision. As a result, you might misjudge the frequency and magnitude of these events. You give greater importance to this information and tend to overestimate the likelihood of similar things happening in the future.[25]

Another example of the availability heuristic involves physical visibility and supermarket shoppers. Assume you are shopping for groceries. What types of products catch your attention? Evidence shows that shoppers tend to buy more products in a supermarket that are displayed at eye level or just below (more available) than those that are more out of the way (less available). The availability heuristic has the power to persuade. Consequently, supermarkets and other retailers can charge manufacturers more if they want their products displayed in these well-placed positions.[26]

The *availability heuristic*, also called the *availability bias*, is a mental shortcut that facilitates decision-making based on information that is easy to recall, widely available, and highly publicized. In other words, this heuristic allows people to judge the likelihood of an event or situation simply based on examples of similar situations that quickly come to mind, allowing them to extrapolate to the situation in which they find themselves. This relation partly happens because of the limitations on memory. Although representativeness and availability seem similar, availability is about particular examples and ease of recall, whereas representativeness is less about specific examples than about stereotypes.[27]

Although the availability heuristic can lead to fast decisions, it can sometimes result in bad judgments. Relying on this heuristic can result in incorrectly assessing the likelihood of events because decision-makers place undue emphasis on information that is readily available. People mistakenly think of things that stand out in their minds as more important in making good decisions or more likely to occur than those that are difficult to imagine or remember.[28] This ease of recall can influence behavior, thus making people predisposed to over-emphasize, overestimate the likelihood, or misinterpret this information. Factors influencing the availability heuristic on people's judgments and decisions include the ability to induce affective or emotional reactions, extremely dramatic events, and recent events.[29]

Here are several examples of the availability bias involving investments. When evaluating stocks, investors tend to over-rate the importance of recent investment news and discount older information. They also are inclined to invest in the highest-performing mutual funds (winners), which are gener-ally the most highly advertised, due to the availability and im-pact of this information. Another example of availability bias involves the financial crisis of 2007–2008. Many investors left the stock market as a result of a steep decline in market prices. Their recent experience led to an upward bias in their expecta-tions of another crisis.

Investors need to be aware that recent, prominent, and emo-tionally charged financial events are readily available and can often dominate their choices. To lessen availability bias, you need to retain a sense of perspective. That is, you should avoid being caught up in the latest news and short-term approaches and focus on the long-term picture. You also need to examine other tools, investment options, and decision-making strat-egies available to you before making a choice. By thoroughly researching your investments, you can better understand the relevance of recent news and act accordingly.

What Role Does Anchoring Play When Making Investment Decisions?

Have you ever considered buying a diamond engagement ring? If so, how much should you pay for the ring? Conventional wisdom suggests spending about two months' salary on the ring. This standard or benchmark is an example of anchoring and represents an irrelevant reference point created by the jewelry industry to increase its profits. The amount spent on an engagement ring should depend on what someone can afford, not on some arbitrary reference point.[30]

Anchoring refers to the tendency to rely on the first number or piece of information as a subjective reference point for making future judgments. Think of anchoring as a "first impression" bias. For example, in a salary negotiation, the person who makes the first offer establishes a range of reasonable possibilities in each person's mind. Once someone forms an initial picture of a situation, seeing other possibilities is more difficult. Thus, any counteroffer is a reaction to that opening offer, which serves as an anchor. Although a popular belief is that an applicant should not make an opening offer, research suggests that view is completely backward. The person who makes a first offer is often better off.

A problem with the anchoring heuristic is that people often have difficulty altering or changing their viewpoints when faced with new information. By being anchored by salient past events, they incorrectly interpret new information through the lens of the original anchor. Sometimes people make adjustments to these imperfect anchors, but these adjustments can also reflect biases.

Anchoring is prevalent in many financial decisions, including investments, and can lead to poor decisions. Here are a few examples. First, investors engaged in anchoring could reject a correct decision such as buying an undervalued investment or selling an overvalued investment. They could also accept an incorrect decision such as ignoring an undervalued investment or buying or holding an overvalued investment.

Another example is when investors latch onto the original price they paid for an asset as a reference point, such as a stock that they acquired at $50 a share. This historical price serves as an anchor. If the stock price declines, those with an anchoring bias tend to hold on to the stock until they get back the original price they paid. They have anchored their fair-value estimate to the acquisition price (a reference point) rather than to fundamentals. Thus, these investors assume greater risk by holding the stock hoping it will return to its purchase price in order to break even.

A third instance involves investing in companies whose stocks have experienced large price drops during a short period. Investors often anchor on the recent high stock price, believing that a price drop affords the opportunity of buying the stock at a substantial discount. Although price declines can sometimes enable investors to take advantage of short-term volatility, such declines often result from a worsening of the stock's fundamentals. By contrast, other investors apply a negative anchor after a market bubble bursts. That is, they anchor to a negative outcome and believe more market declines are coming.

A final example is when people anchor on investment names such as the terms *conservative* or *aggressive*. Not surprisingly, mutual funds include such descriptors. The problem is that the notion of conservative or aggressive could differ markedly between the fund's portfolio manager and its investors.

Although detecting anchoring bias requires awareness, mere awareness is not enough. Overcoming this bias requires engaging in critical thinking and reflecting on one's decision-making history. Another approach is to carefully evaluate an investment's potential by identifying the factors that underlie the anchor and replacing guesswork with quantifiable data.

What Is the Affect Heuristic and How Does It Influence Decision-Making?

Have you ever made decisions that were heavily influenced by your current emotional state? Of course you have. How did that work out for you? Emotions play a critical role in both big and little decisions that you make. Evidence suggests that when you are in a positive emotional state, you are more likely to perceive an activity as having high benefits and low risks. If your emotional state is negative, you are more inclined to see the activity as having low benefits and high risks.[31]

The psychologist Paul Slovic coined the term *affect heuristic* to describe how people let their emotions color their beliefs. An affect heuristic is a mental shortcut in which a person relies on emotion, intuition, and "gut feeling" when making a decision. This fast and frugal heuristic is quick and relatively easy to apply and reduces the cost of searching for and processing information. By contrast, the analytic, rational system of the brain is relatively slow and requires effort. Yet one's feelings and emotional state can influence perceptions and cognitions. Although debate exists about whether emotions enhance or detract from investor decision-making, the overall evidence suggests that, on balance, emotions hinder investors in making effective decisions.[32]

How can the affect heuristic influence investors? If investors have positive or pleasant feelings about something, they are more inclined to perceive an investment as having high returns and low risk. They also are apt to be more confident in evaluating investment options. For example, if investors have strong, positive feelings about a company, they are likely to perceive its stock as less risky and be willing to pay a higher price for it.[33] Hence such investors see high benefits and low risk. Why? They often generalize the good characteristics of a growth company when evaluating it as an investment. As a result, they have a habit of overestimating the likelihood of growth companies being good investments and unknowingly overpay for their shares.[34] A negative emotional state leads people to be more critical when evaluating investments.

In summary, the affect heuristic can strongly influence decisions. Being aware of the proclivity to be swayed by feelings and emotions may enable you to make more objective and clear-minded decisions in the future. Research suggests that third-person self-talks can improve emotion regulation and self-control by facilitating self-distancing and reducing ego-centric bias.[35] Hence, this strategy may prevent bad decisions in the heat of the moment by helping you to remain calm, collected, and level-headed.[36]

What Is Framing and How Can It Influence Decision-Making?

A second key theme in behavioral finance is framing. *Framing* refers to how people react to a particular choice depending on how it is presented. A *frame* is simply the form used to describe a problem or situation. Framing portrays a choice or outcome in terms of its positive or negative consequences, not as good or bad. For example, advertisers use language to frame their messages to influence consumers. They attempt to create a positive emotional frame for the product in the consumer's mind. When advertising a high-end automobile, advertisers use such words as "luxurious," "superb craftsmanship," and "well-appointed" but avoid using terms such as "expensive" and "overpriced." For a lower-priced car, advertisements employ such words as "affordable" and "dependable" instead of "cheap" and "sturdy."[37]

Standard finance assumes that describing the same content in different ways (i.e., using different frames) will not affect how people make judgments or decisions. This assumption of *frame independence* suggests that financial decision-makers view all decisions through the same objective and transparent lens of risk and return. Under the standard finance paradigm, a rational decision-maker should see through the frame, no matter how opaque. A message's framing does not change its meaning or substance, only its form. Thus, standard finance views framing as irrelevant to behavior because people should make the same decisions or have the same preferences across different presentations of the choice.

Yet much evidence suggests that this view does not accurately describe human judgment. People make different choices depending on how a given problem is presented to them. In behavioral finance, framing, or how choices are presented, matters. The *framing effect* is a type of cognitive bias in which people react to a particular choice in different ways depending on its presentation. For example, whether the decision-maker frames a prospect as a gain or a loss, or in terms of probabilities of success or failure, makes a difference. Gain-frame messages promote the benefits of actions and describe a choice or outcome in terms of its positive (gain) features, while loss-frame messages emphasize the consequences of failing to take certain actions or negative (loss) features. People have a tendency to avoid risk when a positive frame is presented but seek risk when a negative frame is presented. This behavior is inconsistent with the standard finance assumption that people are risk-averse regardless of the frame.

For example, people generally prefer taking a sure $1,000 instead of a riskier 50-50 chance at $2,000, reflecting risk aversion for gains. But someone who must either take a certain loss of $1,000 or a 50-50 chance of losing nothing or $2,000 most likely will select the risky alternative. Thus, by framing the same situation in terms of losses, the person prefers the riskier alternative that offers a chance of not losing anything.

What Role Do Biases Play in Behavioral Finance?

The third key theme in behavioral finance concerns biases. In standard finance, people are rational utility maximizers who don't exhibit cognitive biases and aren't swayed by unconscious forces such as emotions and social influences. By contrast, many of the early foundations of behavioral finance are based on cognitive psychology, which focuses on human judgmental processes and financial decision-making under conditions of risk and uncertainty. Cognitive psychology deals with the implications of investor cognitive limitations as well as various heuristics and judgmental biases that lead to decision errors. A *cognitive bias* is a systematic pattern of deviation from a norm or rationality in judgment, which may result in making illogical inferences about other people and situations.

Let's return to the example of how using a heuristic to select a mutual fund can lead to a cognitive bias. Investors often believe that past performance matters more than it does because of a cognitive bias called *recency bias*, which is the tendency to believe what has been happening recently will continue happening in the future. Why? People are apt to more easily remember something that has happened recently than in the past. Consequently, they use recent experience as a baseline for what may occur in the future. Given that mutual fund firms are inclined to advertise their past winners, investors are likely to become more aware of the advertised funds. Despite the SEC requirement that performance advertisements contain a disclaimer warning that "past performance does not guarantee future results," this announcement does not seem to slow down investors from flocking to past winners, as evidenced by the strong positive effect on fund flows. Although recency bias works fine in some situations, it can cause problems involving money and investing.

During the early development of behavioral finance, researchers generally focused on cognitive biases. As time passed, they placed additional importance on emotional and social-cultural influences. *Emotional finance* is a relatively new branch of behavioral finance that explores the role of unconscious processes in driving financial decisions and market behaviors. Thus, although cognitive behavioral finance focuses on how people think, emotional finance emphasizes the unconscious process of investor activity and deals with how people feel. It draws on the psychoanalytical understanding of the mind and dynamic mental states to explain how unconscious processes can drive investment decisions and financial activity.[38]

Emotional finance has many applications in practice. At the individual level, knowledge of the subtle and complex ways feelings determine psychic reality may help people gain a better understanding of how they make asset valuations and investment judgments. Thus, recognizing and understanding unconscious forces can improve the quality of investment decision-making. At a collective level, emotional finance provides a way to understand asset pricing bubbles and associated market phenomena such as the dot-com mania, the real estate bubble, and the Bitcoin phenomenon. A bubble occurs when market participants drive the price of financial and real assets considerably above their intrinsic values. *Intrinsic value*, also called *fundamental value*, refers to an investor's perception of the inherent value of an asset determined through fundamental analysis without reference to its market value. This value may or may not be the same as the current market value. Bubbles can't occur in rational markets, but they can occur in markets affected by biases.

What Role Do Inefficient Markets Play in Behavioral Finance?

The fourth key theme in behavioral finance is inefficient markets. An important paradigm in standard finance is the notion of market efficiency. In an efficient market, the price of each security equals its intrinsic or fundamental value. For example, an efficient stock market would price every stock correctly. Rational traders are assumed to exploit any mispricing for their own profits, which brings the market rapidly into equilibrium. In standard finance, efficient financial markets are a simple place. In reality, financial markets are complex. Advocates of behavioral finance contend that the *efficient market hypothesis* (EMH) is based on a counterfactual assumption about human behavior—rationality. According to the EMH, existing share prices always incorporate and reflect all relevant information, which implies that "beating the market" is impossible. Behavioral finance asserts that errors, decision frames, emotions, and biases of individuals and groups of people lead to market prices deviating from intrinsic values. Further, the limits of arbitrage may prevent rational investors from correcting those price deviations. Behavioral finance provides an alternative view of financial markets in which systematic and significant deviations from market efficiency are expected to persist for long periods of time.

What Developments Contributed to the Early Growth and Eventual Acceptance of Behavioral Finance?

The origins of behavioral finance stem from seminal research, especially in cognitive psychology, during the 1960s and 1970s. Behavioral finance started to take off when economists became aware of advances made by psychologists that could be applied to their field. The contributions of earlier pioneers played a central role in the field of behavioral finance.

In the early 1980s, researchers began to combine the research ideas and methodologies of psychology with specific investment and financial subject matter. Scholars discovered many empirical results that challenged the predictions of standard finance, such as the EMH. During the second half of the twentieth century, the EMH was the dominant theory of financial markets. According to the EMH, existing security prices fully reflect all available information. Given that all participants should act rationally and maximize their financial interests, they should respond to information in a similar manner and make similar decisions. Consequently, any unexploited profit opportunities should not last long in the market, as unbiased rational investors quickly exploit any mispricing for their own profit, thus restoring the true equilibrium price by eventually driving irrational investors out of the market. Although these arbitrageurs should theoretically keep markets efficient, the EMH does not take into account irrationality.

Several market events or developments toward the end of the twentieth century challenged the underlying tenets of the EMH and other traditional financial models. One such event was the Stock Market Crash of 1987, or "Black Monday," which was the largest one-day market crash in history. The crash started in Hong Kong and moved west to Europe, hitting the United States after large declines in other markets. For example, the Dow Jones Industrial Average (DJIA) lost more than 22.6% of its value, or $500 billion, on October 19, 1987. The DJIA is the oldest and best-known stock market index that measures the daily price movements of 30 large American companies. Although many view it as a proxy for general market conditions, it is not the best representation of the entire market. The crash moved to Australia and New Zealand, but was called "Black Tuesday" in those countries because of the time zone difference. By the end of October, stock markets in Hong Kong, Australia, Spain, the United Kingdom, the United States, and Canada had fallen about 45.5%, 41.8%, 31.0%, 26.5%, 22.8%, and 22.5% respectively.[39]

Although the Stock Market Crash of 1987 is mysterious from the perspective of efficient markets, it still would be allowed as a rare statistical event. Yet these losses puzzled many financial economists who believed that such volatility should not occur due to the improved efficiency of information and capital flows. The public generally viewed *program trading* as the primary cause of this crash. Program trading refers to automatic, computerized trading by institutional investors for large blocks of securities. Secondary causes included overvaluation, illiquidity, and market psychology.

Other large bubbles and crashes in the absence of substantial changes in valuation cast doubt on the assumption of efficient markets. For example, a Japanese asset price bubble occurred between 1986 and 1991, resulting in highly inflated real estate and stock market prices. This price bubble burst in early 1992. Characteristics of this bubble included rapid acceleration of asset prices due to overconfidence and speculation, overheated economic activity, and an uncontrolled money supply and credit expansion.

In the United States, the dot-com bubble was a period of excessive speculation occurring roughly between 1997 and 2001, a period characterized by extreme growth in the usage and adaptation of the internet by businesses and consumers. This period witnessed the founding and subsequent failure of many internet-based companies, often called dot-coms. Other companies sustained large declines in market capitalization but survived. The bubble collapsed between 2000 and 2002 as stock prices plummeted, companies folded, investors lost fortunes, and the American economy ultimately slipped into a recession.

Neither the Japanese asset price bubble nor the U.S. dot-com bubble represents realistic assessments of the valuations. Thus, part of the initial attraction for the new behavioral finance field was that market prices did not appear to be fair and that psychology could help explain why prices deviate from fundamental value. Neither the rational person assumption nor the EMH can convincingly explain the causes of these market bubbles and crashes. In fact, bubbles can't exist in rational markets because bubbles imply deviations of prices from intrinsic values.

How Did the Financial Crisis of 2007–2008 Spur the Relevance of Understanding Human Behavior?

The financial crisis of 2007–2008, also called the *global financial crisis*, demonstrated weaknesses inherent in standard finance. It further enhanced the credibility of behavioral finance by offering a painful reminder that psychology and emotions are fundamental to how the financial system functions. Specifically, the financial crisis raised important questions about the rationality of the securities markets. In rational markets, prices should closely track their intrinsic values, resulting in little or no chance of price bubbles. During the period leading to the financial crisis, asset prices, including those in the housing sector, appeared to deviate from their correct values, resulting in subsequent financial crashes around the globe and a recession. The financial crisis refuted the traditional view that even if only some investors are rational, the market will act rationally because arbitrageurs will try to make a profit by shorting overvalued stock and thereby correct mispricing. Hence, the financial crisis provides additional evidence that markets aren't always efficient.

For advocates of efficient markets, the financial crisis highlighted the need to explain why these markets periodically reflect destructive periods of booms and busts. This situation posed a dilemma: EMH advocates could either say the market was efficient and correctly valued before or after the financial crisis, but not both. Implications of the financial crisis are that financial markets are sometimes inefficient and that a need exists to incorporate behavioral finance into economic and financial theories.

The financial crisis also reinforced the notion that investors are hampered by various biases. For example, an emotional bias evident in the price run ups before the financial crisis is *overconfidence*. In terms of investing, overconfidence is the tendency of investors to overestimate their level of skills, expertise, or accuracy when forecasting future stock market performance. Overconfident investors often believe they are better than others at choosing both the best stocks and best times to enter or exit a position. This situation was not the case for many, if not most, investors.

The aftermath of the financial crisis affected individual investors and risk-taking psychology. For example, some investors adopted a more cautious financial psychology and experienced lower levels of risk tolerance and higher degrees of negative emotion and perceived risk. As a result, they tended to underinvest in risky assets such as common stocks and overinvest in safer assets such as cash and bonds. Some people also experienced negative long-term biases after the financial crisis that influenced their overall judgment and decision-making. For instance, after the financial crisis, many developed a strong level of mistrust of financial markets and institutions.[40]

What Are Some Criticisms and Limitations
of Behavioral Finance?

Over its history, behavioral finance has had its share of critics, especially among some traditionalists. One of its harshest critics is Eugene F. Fama, who many view as the father of the EMH. Fama shared the Nobel Memorial Prize in Economic Sciences in 2013. Although standard financial theory can't explain some anomalies, Fama does not advocate abandoning market efficiency in favor of behavioral finance. Instead, he asserts some anomalies found in standard finance are shorter-term chance events that are eventually corrected over time. According to Fama, market efficiency survives the challenge from the literature on long-term return anomalies. He also maintains that many of the findings in behavioral finance appear to contradict each other. Fama suggests that apparent anomalies can be due to methodology and are sensitive to the techniques used to measure them. Much anomaly evidence appears to result from the estimation method for expected returns. When researchers make reasonable changes in technique, many anomalies disappear. Additionally, when testing various strategies using past price data, some will "work" just by chance. But that does not mean those strategies will work in the future. Overall, Fama maintains that behavioral finance appears to be nothing more than a collection of anomalies that can be explained by market efficiency.[41]

Based on his early review of theory and empirical work on efficient capital markets, Fama concludes that evidence supporting the efficient markets model is extensive and contradictory evidence is sparse.[42] In the late 1970s, Michael Jensen, one of the creators of the EMH, stated, "There is no other proposition in economics which has more solid empirical evidence to support it than the Efficient Markets Hypothesis."[43] However, this evidence supporting market efficiency is outdated and has been eroded, as have the theoretical foundations of the EMH. Although some tenaciously cling to the belief that markets are efficient, a growing mountain of evidence contradicts the notion of efficient markets, lending support to the behavioral point of view. Thus, given research advances in behavioral finance over the past several decades, the concept of the EMH has fallen out of favor among many.

Another criticism expressed by Fama is that market efficiency per se is not testable because it is an incomplete hypothesis and can't be proven true or false. Any test of the EMH is also a joint test of an asset-pricing (equilibrium returns) model that defines normal returns. Researchers call this notion the "joint hypothesis problem." Thus, when a model yields a predicted return that differs significantly from the actual return, known as *alpha* in the modeling test, the finding could result from a flawed asset-pricing model or a truly inefficient market.

A third criticism of behavioral finance involves using experimental and survey-based techniques. Fundamental differences exist between research in psychology and finance. Research in psychology generally involves setting up experiments and surveys designed to manipulate a variable that researchers are interested in observing and controlling. With this experimental design, a controlled experimental factor is subjected to special treatment for purposes of comparison with a factor kept constant. The experimental approach has several advantages, such as having control over the variables, providing careful measurement, determining cause and effect relations, and obtaining better results because the experiments can be replicated and results can be checked again.

This research design also has limitations. First, participants know they are in an experiment, which can affect their behavior. Thus, the artificiality of the setting may produce unnatural behavior that does not reflect real life. Second, some testing within psychology uses small or nonrepresentative samples, which makes generalizing the finding to the population difficult. Third, the center of decision-making focuses on individuals, which fails to satisfactorily explain markets and the economic world. Finally, demand characteristics or experimenter effects may bias the results and become confounding variables. By contrast, financial researchers use data of actual decisions made in a real economic setting.

Other criticisms of behavioral finance are that it fails to fully acknowledge and integrate the findings of the allied social sciences, offers a narrow critique of standard finance and economics, and fails to offer viable alternatives to the theories it challenges.[44] The failure to incorporate the many research interests it shares with the allied social sciences leads to rigid separation and boundary enforcement. Behavioral finance needs to strengthen its own core theory and use methodologies appropriate to these theories. Also, proponents of behavioral finance have not developed solutions to all of the problems they are studying. Currently, no unified theory of behavioral finance exists despite much effort to create one. In spite of these criticisms, behavioral finance has made astonishing progress over the past several decades.

Can Investors Exploit Market Anomalies Identified by Behavioral Finance in the Real World?

Researchers in behavioral finance have identified numerous market anomalies that are inconsistent with the paradigm in standard finance. A common belief is that no free rides or "free lunches" are available on Wall Street. Yet the apparent persistence of tradable anomalies in the stock market fascinates many investors. An important question is whether investors can exploit these market anomalies to generate superior risk-adjusted returns after expenses.

Common explanations are that anomalies exist due to either an inadequate asset-pricing model or market efficiency. The persistence of some anomalies for decades suggests that they don't constitute evidence of market inefficiencies. However, even if some markets are generally efficient at pricing securities, pockets of market inefficiency could still exist. Although some anomalies may present intriguing opportunities, they may be difficult or impossible to exploit. According to a behavioral framework, anomalies exist because investors fail to collect and process information rationally due to suffering from various biases leading to mispricing.

Despite the greater acceptance of behavioral finance among investors, evidence suggests that developing a strategy based on market anomalies is typically an unreliable and risky way for investors to reap easy short-term rewards.[45] Several plausible explanations are available to explain the inability to profitably exploit market anomalies. First, the anomaly must be real and repeat itself. Anomalies can appear, disappear, and reappear almost without warning. Second, the returns must be sufficiently large to recoup trading costs and taxes. In practice, anomalies frequently result from large-scale data analysis that examines portfolios consisting of hundreds of stocks that deliver just a fractional performance advantage. Third, an investor would have to properly risk-adjust the returns to determine whether trading on the anomaly enabled the investor to beat the market. Fourth, after identifying an anomaly, the act of exploiting it would reduce and eventually eliminate the size of the pricing error. That is, the costs of implementation can exceed the size of the pricing errors. When including real-world effects such as commissions, taxes, and bid-ask spreads, the presumed benefits often disappear for individual investors. The *bid-ask spread* is basically the difference between the highest price that a buyer is willing to pay for an asset and the lowest price that a seller is willing to accept to sell it. Hence, constructing a portfolio based on anomalies is unlikely to be profitable.

What Insights Does Behavioral Finance Provide into the Volatility Puzzle?

Behavioral finance helps to explain various finance phenomena. One of the more puzzling market anomalies is the *volatility puzzle*, which suggests that stock prices change more than they rationally should.[46] Before going forward, let's define price volatility and fundamental volatility. *Price volatility* is the rate at which a security's price actually increases or decreases. *Fundamental volatility* refers to price changes resulting from the arrival of new information about a firm, such as its revenues, profits, and dividends.

Behavioral finance offers various explanations for excess stock-price volatility including emotions, feedback theory, behavioral biases, and the house money effect. If stock prices are the result of a rational valuation process, then as new information arrives in the market, prices should fluctuate. Whether each new bit of information will be good news or bad news is unpredictable. Therefore, prices should fluctuate randomly. However, stock prices move away from fundamentals for long time periods, but eventually move back. Because price volatility exceeds underlying fundamental volatility, some behaviorists assume that investors' emotions drive the difference.

One of the oldest ideas in behavioral finance, going back three centuries to Holland's tulip mania, is that of price-to-price feedback. That is, prices go up (down) because prices previously went up (down). This phenomenon is called the momentum anomaly. *Momentum* is the tendency of rising asset prices to rise further, and vice versa for falling prices. Numerous studies document this anomalous market tendency. Standard finance theory maintains that, once discovered, anomalies should disappear assuming that markets are efficient and obey certain equilibrium models. Because the momentum anomaly has persisted for decades, this evidence suggests that either standard finance models are wrong or the anomaly persists due to some special conditions.[47]

Another explanation for excess stock-price volatility is that decision-makers exhibit behavioral biases. When faced with a complex decision such as valuing a stock, investors often anchor on the price and changes in the price as indicators of value (i.e., anchoring bias). They also tend to overweight more recent events when making decisions about the future (i.e., recency bias, also called extrapolation bias), forecast the continuance of trends (i.e., overoptimism bias), overweight the value of consensus beliefs (i.e., false consensus bias), focus on similar pieces of information (i.e., limited attention bias), seek confirming evidence (i.e., confirmation bias), and mimic the crowd without taking into consideration their own judgment (i.e., herding bias). Investors may also be overconfident in their ability to forecast the continuation of an apparent market trend (i.e., overconfidence bias). These positive-feedback effects may lead to increasing market prices and potential asset bubbles. In contrast, when stock prices begin to decline, investors tend to exhibit negative feedback effects by focusing on negative information when under stress and overweighing the probability of negative events. In other words, they suffer from *negativity* bias, in which people give more psychological weight to bad experiences than good ones.

A final behavioral explanation for the volatility puzzle is the *house money effect*, which is the tendency for investors to take more and greater risks when investing with profits already earned from their investments. Why? Investors tend to mentally segregate their initial capital from the profits that they have subsequently earned. This situation is known as *mental accounting*. Because they treat their profits as a less important form of money, they tend to take greater risks with them. Consequently, if investors have already made money in the market, they continue to invest at increasingly higher prices, leading to excess stock-price volatility.

How Can Loss Aversion Help to Explain Investors' Behavior When the Market Goes Down?

When stock prices decline, investors tend to become loss-averse. A decline in the value of their portfolios reminds them of their incomplete personal control (i.e., illusion of control bias). Loss aversion helps to explain a common investing mistake: when investors evaluate their stock portfolios, they are most likely to sell stocks that have increased in value or have decreased the least amount. Why? Taking a loss is painful. As a result, people hold on to their depreciating stocks. Over time, this foolish strategy eventually leads to a portfolio consisting of shares that are losing money. Even professional money managers succumb to this bias because they tend to hold losing stocks twice as long as winning stocks. Investors postpone the pain of selling shares that have decreased in value as long as possible because selling makes the loss tangible. As a result, they incur more losses.

2

COGNITIVE BIASES

People are prone to errors and biases that influence their decision-making. These mistakes can lead to bypassing rational thinking and relying on preconceived notions or intuition. Some biases are "hardwired" into the brain. Combining different behavioral biases can create a dangerous mixture that, if consumed, can lead to dumb behavior that sabotages success. As Benjamin Graham, a founder of modern value investing, economist, and professor, once wrote: "The investor's chief problem—and even his worst enemy—is likely to be himself."[1] Overcoming behavioral biases can be very difficult, but recognizing, understanding, and mitigating them can lead to improved decision-making and investment performance.

Today, long lists of biases are available. Few biases exist in isolation because deep interactions occur among them. In fact, some biases overlap or conflict with each other. Although controversy exists on how to classify behavioral biases, one straightforward scheme is to group them into cognitive, emotional, and social-cultural biases. The logic behind this classification is that behavioral bias can result from either internal or external factors. Internal factors include cognitive and emotional biases, whereas external factors involve social or cultural influences. However, these categories are merely a grouping device to provide some semblance of order. This chapter examines cognitive biases and gives both everyday and financial examples, especially involving investments.

What Are Behavioral Biases and Why Are They Important?

You probably think that you make rational decisions on topics ranging from buying a new car to investing for retirement. In many instances, you undoubtedly do. Yet, if you are like most people, you are also prone to numerous biases that result in thinking and acting irrationally.[2] Thus, you probably make some poor financial decisions on a consistent basis.

Paul Samuelson, who was awarded the 1970 Nobel Memorial Prize in Economic Sciences, once said, "Well when events change, I change my mind. What do you do?" Unfortunately, people often don't recognize their biases or mistakes and hence don't change their behavior. Not surprisingly, you probably are more aware of the presence of biases in others than in yourself. The failure to recognize your own biases is itself a *bias blind spot*. The key point is to understand the conditions that get you into trouble, improve decision-making when you can, and avoid the situations when you can't.

Let's look at various examples and types of behavioral biases. Do you have a tendency to take credit for your successes or to lay blame elsewhere for failures? If you do, you are prone to *self-serving bias*. How strongly do others influence your beliefs and actions? For example, do you put money in the same investments your friends do? If so, this bias is called the *bandwagon effect*. Do you place too much emphasis on your own views? If the answer is yes, you are displaying *better than average bias*. Are you inclined to place more value on something you own than something you don't? If so, a bias called the *endowment effect* is in play. Have you ever made a decision, such as making an extravagant purchase, and then regretted it? If you are actively avoiding that regret by finding positives about your poor choice, then you are engaging in *choice supportive bias*. Are you inclined to give more importance to negative experiences or information than to positive ones? If you do, you have *negativity bias*. Do you favor decisions that maintain the existing state of affairs? For example, do you continue to use your same service provider for cell phones, television, internet, and insurance packages despite others being better or cheaper? If you do, you display *status quo bias* because you choose not to change your established choices unless a compelling incentive to change arises. The list of such behavioral biases is practically endless.

A behavioral bias, also called a *psychological bias*, is the inclination to think or feel in certain ways that can lead to systematic deviations from a standard of rationality or good judgment. To deal with too much information, people filter out much of it and select the bits of information likely to be most beneficial in some way. They attempt to simplify information processing by using mental shortcuts called *heuristics* to speed up the process of finding a satisfactory solution, rather than an optimal one, and to ease the cognitive load of making a decision. These simple rules may or may not be effective. To handle the problem of missing information, people fill in the gaps with stereotypes, generalities, prior histories, and the familiar. To avoid paralysis by analysis, people need to act quickly, which leads them to be confident in their abilities, to focus on the immediate, to be motivated to finish things, and to choose the least risky option or the one that preserves the status quo. Finally, to know what needs to be remembered, people focus on bits of information that are most likely to prove valuable in the future, which leads to focusing on generalities and key elements. All of these actions result in biases.

Debate exists about whether some biases are truly irrational or whether they result in useful attitudes or behavior. Nonetheless, some behavioral biases can lead to potentially damaging behaviors, resulting in erroneous decisions or blunders. They are classical forms of dysfunctional psychology that affect human behavior in general as well as how people form their beliefs and make business and economic decisions. These built-in "handicaps" alter how people think and behave and can negatively affect their decision-making. Inherent biases can often lead to harmful outcomes unless something happens to change the course of events. As Walt Kelly wrote in a *Pogo* daily cartoon strip on Earth Day in 1971, "We have met the enemy and he is us." In summary, investor biases can have a substantial impact on financial decision-making.

What Are Cognitive Biases and Their Major Types?

In simple terms, a *cognitive bias* or *error* is a deficiency or limitation in how people think. This behavioral mistake occurs when people are collecting, processing, and interpreting information. The identification of many of these biases stems from *cognitive psychology*, which is the scientific study of the mental processes considered to form human behavior. It explains the systematic errors that people make when making decisions due to cognitive limitations. Although everyone has cognitive biases, they often can be reduced or removed through incentives, nudges, training and education, and following rules. This process is called *debiasing*.

Let's examine two major types of cognitive biases: belief perseverance and information processing. *Belief perseverance* is a psychological phenomenon in which people cling to a previously held belief after receiving convincing evidence that rejects the basis of that belief. Once people have decided that they believe something, they are apt to keep on believing it, even when faced with contradictory evidence. Consequently, they are inclined to accept conclusions that are consistent with their belief systems without challenge and to reject those that are inconsistent, despite their underlying logic and plausibility. An entire class of biases can be lumped into a category called belief perseverance. Common examples include conservatism bias, confirmation bias, self-serving attribution bias, hindsight bias, and illusion of control bias. These biases are all discussed in this chapter.

Belief perseverance biases stem from people attempting to avoid conflicts between their beliefs and reality. When experiencing such conflict, a mental discomfort arises that they often try to resolve in the easiest manner possible. The psychological stress experienced by someone who simultaneously holds two or more contradictory beliefs, ideas, or values is called *cognitive dissonance*. That is, people tend to ignore, reject, or minimize any information that conflicts with a particular belief.

Consider the following example of cognitive dissonance. You consider yourself to be smart but can't believe that you made an ill-advised stock investment. As a result of this dissonance, you are likely to avoid information suggesting you aren't a good investor. Instead you seek out support for the original preferred belief. For instance, you may shift the blame for this decision to your financial advisor who recommended the stock or to factors outside of your control, such as changes in the economy. You want to believe that you make good investment decisions. Thus, when faced with contrary evidence, your brain's defense mechanism filters out contradictory information and alters the recollection of the decision.

Information-processing biases involve errors in how people think when processing information to make decisions. People need to gather and consider information to make behavioral choices consistent with their goals and beliefs. Although much information is irrelevant to making these choices and should be ignored, other information is critical to the decision-making process. The difficult task is paying attention to the important information and discarding the irrelevant information. Prior experiences and even momentary distractions can influence decisions. Such biases may influence the ability to make wise decisions, especially related to financial matters, because of a flawed information analysis process. Examples of information-processing biases include familiarity bias, framing bias, limited attention bias, mental accounting bias, outcome bias, and recency bias. These biases are described in this chapter.

What Is Conservatism Bias and How Can It Affect Financial Decision-Making?

Assume you become aware of some bad news about a company's earnings that contradicts a previous earnings estimate. How are you likely to react? If you are a conservatism-biased investor, you are likely to put more emphasis on your initial beliefs about the outcome and less emphasis on new information. A flaw in the way people think is *conservatism bias*, also called *belief revision bias*. It occurs when people maintain their prior view without properly incorporating new information. That is, people tend to ignore or underweight new information that challenges their original, preexisting information. Why? You are afraid to change your initial impressions based on the previous estimate and act on the new information. If you do react, you may do so slowly. The problem with behaving inflexibly is that new information could signal a change in the underlying value of the firm's stock, which could prove costly if ignored.

Here's another example of conservatism bias. You bought a drug stock anticipating that the company would soon announce regulatory approval of a new drug. However, the company instead announces a delay in approval. If you continue to retain your initial belief about the stock without investigating the new information, you are displaying conservatism bias.[3]

People prone to conservatism bias seek out information and others who confirm their views. Thus, they insufficiently revise their beliefs when presented with new evidence. Conservatism is basically the opposite of representativeness, suggesting that the two principles conflict. That is, representativeness bias refers to overreacting to new information, whereas conservatism bias refers to underreacting to the same information. Thus, some behavioral biases conflict with others.

This belief perseverance bias implies that decision-makers can be slower to change their opinions and react to new, critical information than they rationally should. Why? New information can sometimes be difficult to process. Given a constant barrage of information, differentiating between useless noise and vitally important information can be challenging. A human tendency is to weigh information that is easy to process as more important. However, this leaning is often inappropriate. If the new information involves math or is difficult to uncover, verify, or explain, the weighting of importance should often be higher than new information someone can easily understand. Thus, the reluctance to change beliefs may partly stem from the time, costs, and difficulty of assessing new information.

Conservatism bias is a common explanation for departures from the *efficient market hypothesis* (EMH), which is an important concept in standard finance. According to the EMH, market prices fully, quickly, and correctly reflect all available information. In reality, investors don't always react in proper manner to new information. Moreover, the EMH is only one view about markets. In fact, much evidence suggests that the EMH does not do a good job of describing market behavior.[4] Hence, when confronted with new information inconsistent with earlier views, investors and academics may tenaciously cling to their previous views about the EMH or even ignore the new information. This situation occurred despite mounting evidence that the foundation underlying standard finance was beginning to teeter. Over time, a new finance called behavioral finance emerged as an alternative view of financial markets.[5]

Conservatism bias also helps to explain the underreaction phenomenon, such as the underreaction of stock prices to news of a major earnings surprise. Instead of adjusting their estimates, both analysts and investors overconfidently remain anchored to their prior views of the company's prospects. As a result, they underweight conflicting evidence with their prior views and overweight confirming evidence. Because both analysts and investors interpret a permanent change in the performance of the business as if it were temporary, the price is slow to adjust.

One way to combat conservatism bias is to carefully examine new information to determine its value compared to previous beliefs. If the tendency is to ignore new information because it is difficult to understand, the remedy is either to take the time to understand what the information means or to contact someone who can explain what it means. Another approach is to keep an open mind and replace prior beliefs when confronted with superior evidence to the contrary. A third strategy to reduce conservatism bias is through proper analysis and weighing of new information. For example, you could ask, "How does this new information alter my objectives or forecasts?"

What Is Confirmation Bias and What Are Its Implications?

Assume you believe the market is doing well because of loose monetary policies of the Federal Reserve (Fed), which is the central bank of the United States. *Monetary policy* is the management of a nation's money supply by the government or central bank. *Loose or expansionary monetary policy* occurs when the Fed increases the availability of money and credit in the marketplace to encourage economic growth. If you listen intently to those who agree with this belief but dismiss anyone who disagrees, you are exhibiting confirmation bias.

Confirmation bias, also called *confirmatory bias*, is the predisposition to seek evidence or interpret information in a way that confirms existing beliefs and to discount or disregard conflicting information. This belief perseverance bias is basically wishful thinking, closed-mindedness, and a way to alleviate discomfort. As Jason Zweig, author and *Wall Street Journal* columnist, notes, "In short, your own mind acts like a compulsive yes-man who echoes whatever you want to believe."[6]

Confirmation bias occurs when people filter out potentially meaningful facts and opinions that fail to support their preconceived notions or conclusions. People gather facts and interpret them to support their fixed conclusions. Consequently, they stop gathering information when new evidence validates the views they want to be true, which increases the chance of a bad outcome. In summary, confirmation bias represents a common kind of the fallacy of selective attention in which attention focuses on certain aspects of the argument while completely ignoring or missing others.[7]

Let's consider several examples of confirmation bias. You are evaluating a stock to add to your portfolio. You are likely to gather confirming evidence when making investment decisions rather than evaluate all available information. Thus, you lean toward devoting most of your time to looking for strategies that "work" or evidence that supports your existing investment philosophy. Here is another example of confirmation bias. If you like a company, the tendency is to dismiss negative information as irrelevant or inaccurate. Thus, you may continue to hold a stock whose price is declining far longer than you should. Why? You are likely to interpret news about the company favorably, and even search for information that reinforces the case that the company remains a good investment.

Confirmation bias can be particularly dangerous for investors by holding them back from achieving their full potential and their ability to learn, grow, and improve themselves. One study finds that investors use message boards to seek information that confirms their prior beliefs. In that study, this confirmation made them more overconfident and produced poor investment returns.[8]

Because people are prone to believe what they want to believe, confirmation bias can be difficult to overcome. People naturally seek to confirm their beliefs. Mitigating this bias requires being aware of the danger of confirmation bias, being open to other points of view and new possibilities, and being willing to objectively evaluate one's belief systems. Although actively seeking information that challenges existing belief systems may seem counterintuitive, this balanced, evidence-based investment approach can lead to better-informed decisions.[9] Being able to see things differently requires seeking out and considering sources that look at things differently. Obtaining such evidence could be as simple as reading or listening to some opposing views or asking someone to play devil's advocate. A *devil's advocate* is one who expresses an opinion against a position, not as a committed opponent but to determine the validity of the position. This person acts as a "dissenting voice of reason."[10] Understanding a contrary viewpoint helps the thinking process and provides a good way of determining the coherence of one's viewpoint.

Warren Buffett, one of the most celebrated investors in history, avoids confirmation bias by giving voice to opinions that contradict his own. For example, he once invited a vocal critic who was short-selling his firm's stock to participate in an annual meeting to provide a counterview. *Short selling* refers to selling a security that is not owned by the seller or that the seller has borrowed. An investor motivated to engage in short selling believes that a security is currently overpriced and likely to decline, enabling the investor to buy it back at a lower price to make a profit. Although the critic did not convince Buffett to dump his shares in Berkshire Hathaway, Buffett listened and made a decision based on facts and analysis, not thinking tainted by confirmation bias.[11]

What Is Self-Serving Attribution Bias?

A belief perseverance bias related to confirmation bias is *self-serving attribution bias*, which refers to people's tendency to attribute positive events or outcomes to personal factors, but negative ones to others or to external factors beyond their control. When things go wrong, people look for someone or something to blame, a phenomenon known as *scapegoating*. For example, if an investment turns out to be highly favorable, you are likely to attribute your success to your own knowledge and skill. If the investment fails to meet expectations, you may blame others, such as your financial advisor, or some external factor, such as a news article touting the investment.

This cognitive bias is a defense mechanism resulting from the need to maintain and enhance self-esteem or to perceive oneself in an overly favorable manner. A benefit of this bias is that it leads people to persevere even in the face of adversity. For instance, investors may feel more motivated to keep investing money if they attribute their poor portfolio performance to a weak economy rather than to some personal failing. However, this bias can also mean evading personal responsibility for one's actions, which makes learning and improving more difficult.

Several antidotes are available for dealing with self-serving attribution bias. One approach called *mindful awareness* is to become aware of this bias and to self-correct. Although this remedy is often tricky to accomplish in practice, one strategy to lessen self-attribution bias is to obtain training in behavioral biases. For example, Coursera offers online courses in behavioral finance and various behavioral biases. Another tip is to keep track of personal mistakes and successes, then develop accountability mechanisms, such as seeking constructive feedback from others. Although you may be inclined to trumpet your successes and downplay your failures, you can often benefit from analyzing and correcting your financial mistakes. Everyone makes mistakes, but only the wise learn from them. As Henry Ford, founder of the Ford Motor Company, once observed, "The only real mistake is the one from which we learn nothing." A final suggestion is to try to stay humble regardless of the level of success. Overconfidence in your abilities and overoptimism about future events are frequent enemies of continued investment success. As Humphrey B. Neill, a noted financial author, once wrote: "Don't confuse brains with a bull market." A *bull market* is a financial market of a group of securities in which prices are rising or are expected to rise.

What Is Hindsight Bias and What Are Its Implications for Financial Decision-Making?

Have you ever said to yourself, "I knew that would happen"? Sure you have. Many examples of hindsight bias occur in everyday life and financial situations. For instance, have you ever bet on a sports event, predicting that your team would win by a large margin? If your team actually won, you boasted, "I predicted it!"

Another example involves the financial crisis of 2007–2008. It began with the bursting of an $8 trillion housing bubble. The resulting loss of wealth led to sharp cutbacks in consumer spending. After the bubble burst, many pundits and analysts claimed that signs of this bubble were clear: "Everyone knew it was going to crash" or "Of course the bubble burst." They tried to demonstrate how seemingly trivial events at the time were actually harbingers of future financial trouble. Yet, if the formation of a bubble was so obvious at the time, it probably would not have escalated to that level and eventually burst.

A problematic sibling to confirmation bias is hindsight bias, also known as the "I-knew-it-all-along effect," which is the inclination to see events as more predictable after they have already happened than they really were. By filtering the memory of past events through present knowledge, people perceive actual outcomes as more reasonable, expected, and foreseeable than they really were and give an inflated sense that they saw the result coming. According to the old saying "Hindsight is 20/20," events appear obvious after the fact but were not apparent from the outset. This bias in human thought is a type of "Monday morning quarterbacking" in which an occurrence that was only one of many possible outcomes retrospectively appears inevitable.

Several factors contribute to hindsight bias. First, people are apt to distort or even misremember their earlier predictions about an event. Such memory distortion results in storing the information with the wrong "timestamp" so that a person thinks the knowledge came before the true revelation. Thus, selective memory leads to overestimating what could have been known.[12] Second, people are apt to view events as inevitable. Third, they often assume that they could have anticipated certain events.[13]

Although hindsight bias helps people save face after a bad decision, it can also result in several problems. For example, people may blame themselves for things that they did not predict in advance and consequently may feel responsible or guilty. For instance, someone could invest in the stock of a company that goes bankrupt, resulting in a considerable loss of wealth. Perhaps the most dangerous investing effect of hindsight bias is creating overconfidence in one's judgments and forecasts after a series of good decisions. Such overconfidence can lead to excessive risk-taking because of a false sense of security resulting from past decisions. As an example, investors may allocate too much of their portfolios to one sector because they are overconfident in their predictive ability. Hindsight bias also inhibits learning because it involves distorting past events and hence can get in the way of learning from those experiences and investment mistakes.

Research shows that merely telling people that they should be aware of hindsight bias is ineffective. However, several effective approaches are available to address hindsight bias. One technique is to keep a detailed record or diary of all forecasts and their outcomes.[14] Looking backward, the past may seem as a single line leading to today, but going forward involves many possibilities. Another method to lessen this cognitive bias is to contemplate alternative causal explanations for a given outcome. Considering and explaining how outcomes that did not happen could have happened counteracts the inclination to discount information that fails to fit with one's narrative. This approach to overcoming hindsight bias requires reappraisal of a situation from your perspective at the time.[15] A third approach to reducing hindsight bias is to argue against the inevitability of the outcomes. Using this approach, you can ask yourself to justify your judgments and consider alternative ways things could have turned out.[16]

What Is the Illusion of Control Bias and How Can It Affect Decision-Making?

People have a tendency to overestimate their ability to control events. The illusion of control bias is common in many everyday situations. For example, are you a sports fan? If so, have you ever thought that your actions or rituals affected the game? In reality, they don't. Another illustration involves pushing the door-close button in newer elevators. Typically, doing so does not work because it is on a timer. Although the button only gives the illusion of button-pushers being in control, you may still compulsively press the button. The door eventually closes, reinforcing your perceived power. Similarly, have you ever pushed the crosswalk button multiple times, as if pushing it more times makes the light change faster? It doesn't, but when the light changes, you might attribute the change to the flurry of button pushing.

This belief perseverance bias also may include random events and situations such as effectively rolling dice at the gambling tables and choosing the winning lottery numbers. In these situations, people often treat chance events as controllable. One case in point involves the game of craps. Studies show that gamblers throw the dice harder when they need high numbers and softer for low numbers, illustrating an implicit belief that with "skill" they can somehow control their fortune. A second situation involves those participating in a lottery. Many playing the lottery believe they have more control over the outcome if they chose their numbers rather than having them randomly assigned. That is, gamblers often think they have a greater chance of winning than they actually do when they pick the numbers.[17]

This cognitive bias, called the *illusion of control*, is the tendency for people to overestimate their ability to control or at least influence outcomes or events. The illusion of control can be frustrating and leads to accepting "blame" when doing so is inappropriate. An economic consequence of those suffering from this bias is unnecessarily expending time, money, and mental energy trying to affect outcomes that they can't influence. Illusion of control bias also leads to other well-known behavioral biases, including overconfidence and overoptimism, which are emotional biases. Early success strengthens this illusion. For instance, investors or traders who experience initial success in timing the market may believe that they controlled the outcome and may interpret lucky investment decisions as skill.

Illusion of control bias can also lead investors to trade more than is prudent. According to one study, the more traders think they are in control, the worse their actual performance.[18] This form of dissonant behavior can also lead investors to maintain improper portfolio diversification or to use limit orders and other such techniques to experience a false sense of control over their investments. A *limit order* is a direction that an investor gives to a broker to buy or sell a security or commodity at a specified price or better. This order usually includes an indication of how long it remains in effect.

Active investors who believe that they can consistently outperform the market on a risk-adjusted basis generally suffer from the illusion of control. Although they can control their asset allocation, security selection, and market timing, they can't control the outcomes of these decisions. Given that less than 5% of investors can consistently outperform the market after trading costs, most of these active investors suffer from this illusion. In reality, market success or lack thereof typically results from uncontrollable factors such as corporate performance and general economic conditions.[19]

Dealing with the illusion of control often starts with recognizing the actions possible within your sphere of influence and control and those that are not. You should seek different views before investing and also keep records of investment decisions, including the reasons behind them. Taking these actions should help you determine whether you can accurately predict the market. Unfortunately, you probably can't. Another way of dealing with this cognitive bias is to follow a well-designed investment plan and avoid unnecessary trading.

What Is Familiarity Bias and How Does It Manifest Itself in Investing?

Do you prefer things that are familiar? For instance, you may shop at a certain place, buy a particular brand, or take the same route to work. Although this mindset may be harmless in everyday life, it can affect your financial health and lead to substandard returns. In the investment realm, *familiarity bias* is the propensity to make investment decisions based on being aware of an investment option such as the name or reputation of the company or its products. Not surprisingly, the brain uses the familiarity shortcut to evaluate investments.

Here are two investing examples of familiarity bias. Although the stocks of hundreds of electric utility companies are available for investment purposes, investors are apt to buy stock in their local utility because it is more familiar. When presented with two mutual funds with similar characteristics, they are likely to pick the more familiar fund.

Investing in what is familiar is not necessarily an investment strategy that is likely to yield the most investing success. Investors can financially lose out by sticking with what they know, despite better options being available. The popular wisdom of "invest in what you know" ignores the role of serious fundamental stock research. Investors might be better served by buying into what they can learn.

Fundamental analysis is a method of evaluating a security in an attempt to measure its intrinsic value, by examining related economic, financial, and other qualitative and quantitative factors. *Intrinsic value* is a security's actual value based on both tangible and intangible factors. This value may differ from the security's current market price.

As Peter Lynch, who once ran the Magellan Fund, notes, "People buy a stock and they know nothing about it. That's gambling and it's not good."[20] This observation mirrors one of legendary investor Warren Buffett's investing rules: "Never invest in a business you can't understand." To know a company is to deeply understand the inner workings of the business and to operate within your "circle of competence."

Various institutional and behavioral explanations of this information-processing bias are available. In comparing domestic to international asset holdings, some institutional factors limit investors from diversifying into unfamiliar foreign assets, such as currency risk, asymmetric information, corporate governance, and weak property rights. Behavioral explanations include overconfidence in predicting familiar asset returns, preferring local assets to avoid regret, and viewing familiar assets more favorably due to patriotism and social identification.[21]

Familiarity bias manifests itself in different ways when investing. Some people overinvest in their company's stock through incentive stock plans or their employer's 401(k) plan. Investors are also likely to prefer local assets with which they are more familiar (*local bias*) and portfolios tilted toward domestic securities (*home bias*). Still other investors buy stocks of companies whose products they like or use frequently.

Although familiarity breeds investment, it can also lead to investment problems. Perhaps the most important concerns involve underestimating risk and having suboptimal portfolios due to a lack of diversification. Investors exhibiting familiarity bias lean toward overweighting their portfolios with familiar assets, resulting in riskier portfolios. Yet they perceive familiar assets as having an inverse relation between risk and expected return. That is, they perceive highly familiar assets as possessing lower risk and higher expected return, which is inconsistent with financial theory.[22]

To combat familiarity bias, you should expand your portfolio allocation decisions to gain risk reduction and wider diversification by looking beyond the familiar. This approach often requires diversifying not only across asset classes but also geographically both at home and abroad. Doing so should reduce volatility over the long term. Thus, a drawback of just investing in familiar companies is the opportunity cost of not owning companies that are not yet well known. Another approach to lessening this bias is to create checks and balances when investing by using a competent person such as a financial advisor as a sounding board before making investment decisions.

What Is Framing Bias and How Does It Affect Financial Decisions?

Framing bias is the propensity to process and react to information differently depending on how the choices are framed. Framing occurs in all aspects of life. Let's begin by taking a literal view of a frame. Does the frame influence how you view a picture inside the frame? The answer is probably yes. In his book *Choke*, American author Chuck Palahniuk notes, "It's funny how the beauty of art has so much more to do with the frame than the artwork itself." Advertisers and marketers use framing to present information in a manner intended to influence how others interpret that information. For example, consider advertisements for hamburger from two grocery stores. One states, "This beef is 90% lean" (a positive frame), whereas the other says, "This beef is 10% fat" (a negative frame). If the price is the same at both stores, which hamburger would you likely prefer? Most people would choose the hamburger advertised using the positive frame. Although the substance is the same in both advertisements, the frame differs.

Investors are also susceptible to framing, as shown by the following example:

A. An investment increases by $5,000 over the course of a year, but loses $2,000 of that gain due to year-end market volatility.
B. An investment increases by $5,000 over the course of a year, but results in a $3,000 gain despite a market downturn near year-end.

Which option would you choose? If you are like most people, you prefer scenario B because it is presented as a gain instead of a loss—despite the outcomes being the same. This positive frame is more psychologically appealing.

A key issue with this information-processing bias is that it can influence decisions for better or worse. Differences in framing change the weight given to certain factors and may draw attention to different aspects of outcomes. Choices often depend on their framing. The framing of a question can lead to leaning toward a risky or a conservative outcome. Positive versus negative framing may trigger large differences in responses. When events are framed positively, people generally choose the certain event over the gamble even if the gamble yields an equal or greater expected value. They also are likely to choose a positively framed gamble over one negatively framed although they yield the same expected value.[23]

Both form and substance can influence financial behavior. However, as former President Ronald Reagan once noted, "Form and substance are opposite ends of the same coin." The form used to describe a specific problem or decision situation is its *frame*. If the form affects behavior, this is called *frame dependence*. Framing bias occurs when someone processes the same information differently depending on how it is presented and received. As an example, an investor may be alarmed when his financial advisor informs him that his portfolio has a 20% chance of losing money during the next year, but feels optimistic if he is told the same portfolio has an 80% chance of making money during the same period. People should be aware of how information is presented in order to persuade them to take a certain action. Governments and other organizations sometimes try to "nudge" people toward better choices by how they present information.

Let's examine framing-dependent behavior in the context of *house money*, which is the tendency to take more and greater risks when investing with profits. According to the *house money effect*, investors are more disposed to buy higher-risk stocks after a profitable trade. Similarly, gamblers who have won money are likely to increase their risk-taking behavior with their recent profits. Why? In both cases, the investor or gambler has compartmentalized, or framed, money into excess (house money) and nonexcess (the investor's money). Keeping capital separate from recent profits leads the investor or gambler to view these profits as disposable. Such framing contributes to taking greater risks with the money. The house money effect is also a type of *mental accounting*, which is the tendency for people to separate their money into different accounts based on such subjective criteria as the money's source and its intended use.

Framing bias can also alter a portfolio's asset allocation strategy by influencing investors to deviate from their target asset allocations. A new potential investment may look attractive in isolation. But this individual investment frame ignores how the potential investment contributes to the expected return and diversification of the portfolio. Analyzing the potential investment through a portfolio frame allows one to fully understand how it would affect portfolio performance.[24]

You need to hone your skills by recognizing how relevant information is framed. You can lessen framing effects by seeing through the frame and looking at things more objectively. This task is difficult because others often try to "nudge" you into a certain direction or decision through the way they present information. For instance, mutual funds try to nudge potential investors into their high-performing funds by advertising and presenting them in positive ways. Another approach to avoid framing bias is for you to focus on total returns and risk instead of on gains or losses. A final strategy is to reframe the issue. For example, suppose you have a large position in a stock with a substantial unrealized loss but you refuse to sell it until the price recovers. Have you ever said, "If the price would just go up to what I paid for it, I'd sell it!" If so, you should ask yourself: "Would I buy that stock today?" Typically, the answer is no. By keeping the stock, you are actually making a decision to buy it at the current prices. By reframing the decision as a buy instead of a sell, you are more likely to reject the "buy" decision and sell the stock despite incurring a loss.[25]

What Is Limited Attention Bias and How Can It Affect Decision-Makers?

Suppose you are thinking about investing in a stock mutual fund. Given the many funds available, which one are you likely to choose? If your response is similar to many individual investors, you are likely to prefer a stock mutual fund that has recently been performing well, despite the fact that past performance may not be indicative of future results. Why? Fund companies realize that people have an attentional bias toward past performance, so they advertise their best-performing funds. Attentional bias prompts investors to cling to the past and to the familiar. Thus, from a marketing perspective, promoting exceptional past returns is likely to boost fund inflows by attracting attention to these funds.

People often face a vast amount of information when making decisions, but have a finite amount of attention to devote to the process. When they split their attention, performance suffers. As Howard Rheingold, an American writer, critic, and teacher, notes, "Attention is a limited resource, so pay attention to where you pay attention." For example, a driver who is listening to the radio and texting is unlikely to do any of these activities very well. Various psychological constraints affect how much people pay attention to particular information. The factors include the presence of distracting stimuli, the salience and availability of the information, and the ease of processing the information. As a result, people make decisions based on the limited knowledge they accumulate. *Limited attention bias,* also called *attentional bias,* is the inclination to pay attention to some things while simultaneously ignoring others. As a result of this bias, people neglect relevant warning signs, which can lead to mistakes.[26]

This information-processing bias has implications for investors. For example, when selecting mutual funds, investors generally pay more attention to front-end loads and recent fund performance and less attention to operating expenses, 12b-1 fund marketing fees, and back-end loads, even though they are just as important. A *front-end load* is a commission or sales charge applied at the time of the initial purchase of a mutual fund. Because it is deducted from the investment amount, this fee lowers the size of the investment. A *back-end load* is a fee that investors pay when selling mutual fund shares. This fee amounts to a percentage of the value of the shares sold. Attraction to high-performing funds could result in *herding behavior*, in which investors mimic the behavior of others who are also relying on the same information. Additionally, investors who gravitate toward certain attention-grabbing events such as news about a stock, abnormal trading volume, and extreme returns often become buyers after these events.[27] This bias can lead them to make bad choices.

Limited attention bias also has extensive effects on the capital markets. Evidence shows that when investors are less attentive to publicly available information, a greater underreaction to public information occurs. One such example is the postearnings announcement drift (PEAD) anomaly in which prices underreact to earnings news.[28] In financial markets, an *anomaly* refers to a situation when a security or group of securities performs contrary to the notion of efficient markets, where security prices are assumed to reflect all available information at any point in time. Limited attention can also explain the *momentum anomaly*, which is the premise that what was strongly going up in the past will probably continue to go up. Evidence suggests that momentum is stronger for low-attention stocks such as small stocks and stocks with low analyst coverage.[29]

Being aware of these attention limitations is the first step toward mitigating their negative consequences. Learning to research and evaluate securities that are not highly publicized is another important step toward avoiding limited attention bias. Finally, you should rely on multiple sources of information and not let media noise affect your investment decisions.

What Is Mental Accounting and Why Can It Be Detrimental to Financial Health?

Do you separate your money into "buckets"? One money bucket may be for living expenses and another for retirement. Other common buckets are for emergency savings, college education, and vacations. If you do this, you are engaging in mental accounting, which is a type of information-processing bias. Although these mental categories may seem rational, they are often arbitrary and misleading. In investing, money is money regardless of the source or the bucket into which it is placed.

Mental accounting is the propensity for people to separate their money into different accounts based on various subjective criteria, such as the source of the money or its intended use. As a consequence, they are prone to irrational decision-making in their spending and investment behavior. Based on this economic concept, established by Richard H. Thaler, people categorize their assets into separate mental accounts or "buckets" and thus spend or allocate funds differently.[30] Thaler won the Nobel Prize in 2017 for behavioral finance contributions, particularly for framing choices in ways that help people make better decisions. When using separate mental accounts, people view and assess individual assets separately instead of as a part of a total portfolio, which can lead to irrational behavior. For example, someone may have a special "money jar" for a vacation while still carrying substantial credit card debt with high interest charges. In some cases, however, investors can benefit from this behavior. For instance, earmarking money for retirement could avoid spending it frivolously.

Thaler offers an example based on Daniel Kahneman and Amos Tversky's theory of loss aversion. Suppose that an investor owns two stocks—one with a paper gain and the other with a paper loss—and must sell one of them to derive cash. Which stock should the investor sell? The rational choice would be to sell the loser because doing so not only provides tax benefits but also recognizes that the losing stock is a weaker investment. Yet mental accounting separates the stocks into winners and losers and is biased toward selling the winner. Why? By selling the winner, the investor avoids the pain of selling the loser, which could be hard to bear. Thus, combining mental accounting with loss aversion can lead investors astray with their decisions.

Examples of mental accounting abound in everyday life. For example, research indicates that people are willing to spend more when they pay with a credit card rather than with cash.[31] People are also inclined to spend their tax refunds and bonuses differently than how they spend their normal wages. That is, they often view the refund as "found money" and spend it on less thoughtful purchases. Additionally, people view money earned from a job differently from funds obtained from capital gains from an investment, lottery winnings, or funds received from an inheritance. Some investors view an arbitrary amount of their investment capital as "play money," which they are more comfortable using on speculative and uncertain things. Similarly, many investors consider unrealized gains and losses as less important than realized ones. A *realized gain or loss* refers to profits or losses from completed transactions. An *unrealized gain or loss* refers to profits or losses that have occurred on paper but not realized because the investment is still held. As a result, placing money in separate mental accounts results in making different decisions about these accounts.

Treating money in separate "pockets" as distinctly different is economically irrational because these pockets are self-created, illusory, mental categories. Think about mental accounting as "two-pocket" theory. A dollar in your right pocket is worth exactly the same as a dollar in your left pocket. Money is a fungible commodity. That is, money raised for one purpose can easily be used for another. Yet people often violate the fungibility principle. The source of the money should have no effect on where to spend it.

Mental accounting puts portfolios in layers. For example, an *investment pyramid* is a strategy that allocates assets according to the relative safety and soundness of investments. The bottom of the pyramid consists of low-risk investments (e.g., money market securities and bonds), the middle portion contains growth investments (e.g., large-cap stocks, mutual funds, and real estate), and the top has speculative investments (e.g., derivatives and collectibles).[32] Mental accounting fosters a matching between financial goals and a level of the pyramid. Although this approach allows investors to assess and adjust the risk of their portfolios, it ignores the diversification interaction between the layers. Thus, investors sometimes make decisions about individual accounts in their portfolio without considering the relation with other accounts, which results in a suboptimal portfolio.[33]

Several strategies are available to lessen the pitfalls of mental accounting, but some are more attractive than others. For instance, Richard H. Thaler suggests that an alternative to having mental accounts is to consciously ask what every purchase is worth and compare it with every other purchase. Taking this approach could be tedious and is probably unrealistic for most people. A more practical strategy is to develop a written financial budget that translates mental accounts into something that is tangible. A third approach is to focus on the entire portfolio instead of separate "buckets," deploy capital optimally, and avoid squandering money due to mental accounting. A fourth scheme is to get an accountability partner to serve as a sounding board for various expenditures and investments. In finance, an *accountability partner* is someone who provides feedback, potential advice, and support to help a person reach financial goals, keep a commitment, or make good financial decisions. An accountability partner assumes the role of a trusted confidant or a mentor who can provide guidance and motivation.

What Is Outcome Bias and What Problems Does It Pose to Investors?

Let's consider a hypothetical story. Assume that a million monkeys are buying and selling stocks randomly. Periodically, they are evaluated on their performance. Because the trades are random, some monkeys will make a profit in the short term while others will lose money. Those making a profit can stay and continue trading stocks but those incurring a loss are sent home. Over time, fewer and fewer winning monkeys remain until a single monkey is left. Somehow this monkey has managed to choose the right stocks and become a billionaire. Based on this outcome, this brilliant monkey has apparently discovered a secret to successful stock investment. Right? Not really. The monkey was simply lucky. This monkey story illustrates outcome bias.[34]

Outcome bias is the tendency to judge a decision by the final result, whether that outcome occurred by chance or through a sound decision-making process. After making a decision, people typically don't examine the conditions existing at the time of the decision but evaluate performance based on whether the end result was positive or not. When a good outcome occurs, the tendency is to judge the entire effort positively. Yet, if the end result is negative, perhaps for reasons unrelated to the process, a sound decision process may be criticized. Although process and outcome should be evaluated separately, this situation is rarely the case.[35] For instance, an investor decides to invest in oil stocks after learning that a colleague made a large return on such an investment. Instead of evaluating the factors that could have resulted in the colleague's success, such as the state of the overall economy or supply and demand within the energy sector at the time, the investor focuses on the money made by the colleague.

Have you ever judged a decision based on its outcome, not on how you made the decision in the moment? If so, you are guilty of outcome bias. For example, just because you won money on a trip to Las Vegas does not mean that gambling was a smart way to use your money. As Hunter S. Thompson, an American journalist and author, once noted, "There are many harsh lessons to be learned from the gambling experience, but the harshest one of all is the difference between having fun and being smart."

A problem with this information-processing bias is that luck or conditions outside of the person's control could play a role in how things turned out. Another problem with outcome bias is that it can lead to repeatedly making poor decisions. People make this mistake because they incorporate currently available information when evaluating a past decision. Lessening the influence of outcome bias involves focusing on the quality of the decision-making process and ignoring information collected after the fact. An important lesson is to avoid judging a decision based purely on its result, especially when randomness and outside forces play a role.

What Is Recency Bias and How Can It Affect Investment Performance?

Some people focus on "what's happened lately" when evaluating or judging something. In early 2009, the stock market had experienced severe losses for several years, and many investors abandoned the market, having mentally extrapolated those losses into the future. Subsequently, the market staged a dramatic rebound that continued for many years. This substantial upward market movement enticed more timid investors to reenter the market based on this recent performance. This example illustrates recency bias.

Recency bias refers to the tendency to overemphasize more recent data. That is, investors tend to evaluate their portfolio performance based on recent results or on how they perceive these results. Strong memories of the recent past can subconsciously distort judgment. This information-processing bias often stems from the fact that people can more easily remember something that occurred recently than something that happened a while back. Thus, they view new information—which is more recent—as more important than older information.

Examples of recency bias abound in behavioral finance. For instance, when markets are rising, falling, or remaining calm, investors expect more of the same. Using recent experience as the baseline for what is likely to happen in the future works fine in many situations, but it can cause problems when involving money and investing. Periods of large market moves often exacerbate recency bias. To illustrate, when the market is down, many investors are convinced that it will not turn around. They cash out their portfolios and hold their funds in cash or in low-yielding short-term investments. This situation occurred during the lows of the financial crisis of 2007–2008. As a result, many investors missed out on the eventual upturn in the market.

Other examples of this bias are the recent housing crisis and other market bubbles and crashes. Before the housing crisis, housing prices rose rapidly. Many homebuyers ignored historical returns and viewed the current trend as normal. They did not worry that the house was outside of their price range because they anticipated being able to sell it at a higher price if they encountered difficulty making the payments. This belief was a tragic mistake for many homebuyers who found their mortgage "underwater" during the housing crisis. The term *underwater* refers to a mortgage on the house that is larger than the free-market value of the house. Housing prices in the United States peaked in early 2006 and started to decline in 2006 and 2007. When the housing bubble burst, underwater mortgages became commonplace and, combined with a bad economy, resulted in many foreclosures.

In these examples, decision-makers gave less weight to past events, such as historical market downturns, and assumed that more recent events, such as the upside of asset bubbles, were representative of what to expect in the future. Such incorrect conclusions can ultimately lead to faulty decisions about how markets behave. Not surprisingly, individual investors assumed too much risk at the tail end of a bull or rising housing market. Evaluating portfolio performance based on recent results can cloud judgment and lead to incorrect conclusions that ultimately result in poor decisions about future market behavior. Tomorrow's markets may not look like today's markets. Investors afflicted with recency bias may stay in well-performing investments despite warning signs, such as historical or relative high valuation. Recency bias could also keep investors from buying when market prices are low due to falling prices. Extrapolating recent events into the future can ultimately lead to incorrect decisions about how the market behaves. As a result, investors make the mistake of overbuying current outperforming assets and underowning current underperforming assets.

On average, investors who buy retail mutual funds do much worse than the average mutual fund performance. How is this possible? Investors exhibit poor timing skills. Recency bias helps to explain this outcome. These investors tend to invest after good periods and withdraw funds after bad periods. Money tends to flow into stocks near market highs and to exit close to market lows. Buying high and selling low is a very bad investment strategy! Both behaviors are exactly the opposite of the correct course of action. Thus, recency bias can unduly affect your investments. The media and corporate releases of information reinforce recency bias because investors remember and overweight recent events or experiences as part of the decision-making process. One of the best defenses against recency bias is to maintain a long-term investment plan.

How Did the Financial Crisis of 2007–2008 Affect Investor Risk Tolerance and Behavioral Biases?

When the stock market or economy is down, does this affect the amount of risk that you are willing to take? For many people, the answer to this question is yes. Economic shocks such as the financial crisis of 2007–2008 can affect risk toler- ance and change behavior.[36] This crisis has had a long-term impact on risk tolerance, especially on millennials, those born from the early 1980s to the 1990s and sometimes the early 2000s. Younger investors are more sensitive to financially vol- atile markets than are older investors, such as Gen Xers and baby boomers, because they have less investment history. Additionally, the beliefs of younger people are more flexible and influenced by experience. For example, millennials came of age during financially unstable times, namely the financial crisis of 2007–2008, which was the worst economic crisis since the Great Depression. The financial crisis affected the mindset of millennials and provided a profound reality check for them. This experience resulted in a shift by many millennials to a lower risk tolerance and increased prudence due to having experienced inferior stock market performance. Taking lower levels of risk typically leads to lower expected returns, and thus can negatively affect future wealth. This shift is reflected in the long-term reduction in millennials' equity allocations and a corresponding increase in the allocation to cash and debt securities.[37]

The financial crisis also affected various behavioral biases, including anchoring, recency bias, worry, loss aversion, status quo bias, and mistrust. Many investors are anchored on poor financial performance due to recency bias. As a result of the financial crisis, they realized severe losses, whose impact was both financial and emotional. As the level of worry increased, their attention shifted to downside risk due to *loss aversion*, which refers to people's tendency to prefer avoiding losses to acquiring equivalent gains. After the financial crisis, many in- vestors suffered from status quo bias in which they no longer wanted to invest in common stocks and avoided managing their investment portfolios to escape reliving past experience. The financial crisis also led to a heightened level of mistrust of financial institutions and markets. Considerable time could be required to restore this trust.[38]

How Do Different Behavioral Investor Types Affect Behavioral Biases?

Do you have a behavioral investor type? If so, what is it? Most investors can be classified into certain categories but probably are unware of what they are. The importance of knowing your behavioral investor type (BIT) is that it can help you identify behavioral biases associated with a specific type.

Behavioral biases affect all investors and can vary depending on their behavioral type. Michael Pompian, an investment advisor and author, classifies investors into four behavioral investor types: preserver, follower, independent, and accumulator.[39] Each BIT is characterized by a specific risk tolerance level and a primary type of bias—either cognitive or emotional. Emotional biases drive the least (preserver) and most (accumulator) risk-tolerant BITs, while cognitive biases affect the two BITs (follower and independent) in between these two extremes.

- **Preserver.** A *preserver* is an investor who emphasizes financial security and preserving wealth instead of taking risks to grow wealth. Preservers approach investing in a deliberate and cautious way and have a lower than average risk tolerance. They are loss averse and are deliberate in their decision-making because of their concern for making a wrong decision. Their dominant bias types are emotional in nature and are characterized by loss aversion and status quo risk. Preservers are particularly concerned with short-term performance and losing what they had previously gained.
- **Follower.** A *follower* is an investor who often lacks interest in money management and investing and seeks advice from others, typically friends and colleagues. Followers lean toward pursuing a passive investing style because they generally don't have their own ideas about investing. They have cognitive biases relating to following behavior with the most impactful biases being

recency and framing. Although their level of risk tolerance is typically lower than average, followers often think that this level is higher than its actual level. As followers, they sometimes regret being part of the latest investment fad because they entered the market at the wrong time, when valuations were high.

- **Independent.** An *independent* is an investor who is actively engaged in the investment process and has original ideas about investing. Consequently, independents act decisively and are analytical, critical thinkers. Their level of risk tolerance is generally above average. Independents are subject to cognitive biases relating to the pitfalls of doing their own research, including confirmation and availability bias.

- **Accumulator.** An *accumulator* is an investor who focuses on accumulating wealth and is confident in the ability to do so. These investors are actively engaged in decision-making and want to control the investment process. They have a high tolerance for risk-taking. Accumulators often suffer from emotional biases relating to overconfidence and the illusion of control.

Does Knowledge of Cognitive Biases Result in Less Biased Financial Decisions?

Knowledge of cognitive biases is only a starting point in making less biased financial decisions. Everyone suffers, often unknowingly, from behavioral biases that affect sound judgment. Experienced investors are well aware that self-control and self-knowledge are critical to successful investing. In fact, Warren Buffett has said that discipline and the "right temperament" are more important than IQ when investing. Nonetheless, even the most analytical thinkers struggle with self-control. Having knowledge can be helpful in getting off the self-destructive path that sends people astray in their financial lives. However, eliminating all cognitive biases is all but impossible. Few investors never deviate from optimal behavior. Why? For one reason, the brain filters information that it receives in relation to a person's memories. Awareness of one's cognitive biases does not ensure changes in behavior. Nonetheless, people should recognize their biases and be vigilant so that they are not led into poor decisions.

People need to be aware of the *behavioral gap* between what they should do and actually do. Although awareness may lead to a slight improvement in actions and decisions, any effect is probably temporary because the stimuli for the biased action have not been changed or removed. According to Nathaniel Branden, an American psychotherapist and writer known for his work in the psychology of self-esteem, "The first step toward change is awareness. The second step is acceptance." Thus, merely informing people of their adverse behavioral proclivities is rarely effective in combating them. Mitigating these biases requires admitting these biases and then developing and effectively executing a plan to overcome them. Simply knowing about your biases does not necessarily result in changing behavior any more than knowing that you are overweight results in you changing your eating habits. Both require acting upon awareness and knowledge. A major challenge is to avoid the superficial application of behavioral finance. Avoiding this problem requires in-depth knowledge of the field and a solid grasp of the theoretical underpinnings of its more technical aspects.[40]

How Can People Cope with Cognitive Biases in Investment Decision-Making?

Although people can be effective money managers, they often get in their own way. That is, behavioral biases can get the best of them from time to time. Although some cognitive biases can be beneficial, these deep-rooted mental habits often lead to making irrational decisions that can hurt investor portfolios. Behavioral finance identifies and describes cognitive errors, but it provides few remedies. That is, behavioral finance essentially offers a diagnosis but often without a prescription. In fact, when asked what could be done to overcome behavioral biases, Nobel Prize winner Daniel H. Kahneman, one of the founders of behavioral finance, replied: "Very little; I have 40 years of experience with this, and I still commit these errors. Knowing the errors is not the recipe to avoiding them."[41]

A major challenge to achieving investment success is to understand and mitigate behavioral biases. Yet investors often have difficulty recognizing much less overcoming their biases. Why? Even the smartest people exhibit biases in judgments and decisions. Others often don't think they are susceptible to such biases and hence are unable to recognize that they suffer from the same cognitive distortions that plague others. Therefore, they don't do anything to address their biases. Another reason is that changing a bias in isolation ignores the complexity of human behavior. Additionally, some behavioral biases conflict with and are related to others. Finally, those using behavioral finance often fall prey to superficial approaches or inappropriate applications of financial theory.

Here are some general suggestions for trying to counter behavioral biases. The first step in dealing with biases is to bring them from the subconscious to the conscious level. Without being aware of and understanding these biases, you have little hope of building systems to cope with them. As an analogy, if someone has bad breath and is unaware of it, this individual is unlikely to do anything about it and may continue to offend others. One way to gain this awareness is to work with a knowledgeable advisor or an accountability partner. Another way is to gain training and education about behavioral biases. However, awareness by itself does not lead to change. Believing that sheer force of will can overcome such biases is foolish. Major incentives and peer pressure are often required to modify behavior by reducing behavioral biases.

The next action-oriented step is to follow a disciplined investment process resulting in the development of an investment plan. This process should be data driven, not noise driven. An investment plan begins with specifying your investment goals, which requires understanding your risk tolerance and return expectations. A systematic asset allocation is also needed to balance risk and create diversification. *Asset allocation* refers to implementing an investment strategy that tries to balance risk versus reward by adjusting the percentage of each asset in an investment portfolio based on an investor's risk tolerance, goals, and investment time frame. Additionally, the investment plan should have built-in accountability mechanisms with quantitative investment criteria to help monitor decisions and to protect against biases. Finally, your plan should follow fundamental investing principles to ensure appropriate diversification, periodic review, and portfolio rebalancing.[42] Following these simple steps can produce remarkable results. As Warren Buffett notes, "It is not necessary to do extraordinary things to get extraordinary results."

3

EMOTIONAL BIASES
AND SOCIAL-CULTURAL
INFLUENCES

Have you ever made an investment decision based on how you feel about a company, its products, or its leadership? If so, you may suffer from an *emotional bias*, which is a distortion in perception and decision-making due to emotional factors. It relates to how people feel. People are more inclined to believe something that has a positive emotional effect, giving a pleasant feeling, and are hesitant to accept hard facts that are unpleasant, resulting in mental suffering. Emotions can strongly influence economic behavior and decision-making. For example, emotions are useful in explaining asset bubbles and market-related phenomena such as the dot-com mania in 2000 and the financial crisis of 2007–2008. An *asset bubble* is when the price of an asset such as housing, stocks, or gold becomes overinflated.

Psychological influences on investor decision-making extend beyond how investors think and feel. Investors don't make decisions totally based on internal inputs. Do you tend to be influenced by the investing action of your friends, neighbors, or relatives? As social creatures, people are influenced by how others behave. Therefore, behavioral bias may also result from external factors called *social* or *cultural bias*. These social-cultural influences include the media and the internet, as well as friends, colleagues, culture, and other factors. One type of social bias is *herding behavior*, which occurs when individuals mimic the actions of a larger group. For example, investors frequently gravitate to the same or similar investments because many others are investing in them. Such herding behavior can result in bubbles in asset prices as well as panics and crashes. This chapter examines emotional and social-cultural influences on decision-making, especially investing, and how to correct such mistakes.

How Do Emotions Play a Role in Investing?

Can you remember a time when emotions influenced your financial decisions? What was the result? If you are like most people, you can't simply turn your emotions on and off when making decisions, especially involving money. Obviously, people don't make all investment decisions based on rational decision-making using in-depth analysis and financial models. They often make decisions based on behavioral biases, including those associated with emotion. Thus, understanding the role of emotions in the investing process offers a complementary perspective to rational decision-making. People who are otherwise rational in everyday matters may act irrationally and be ruled by their emotions when facing investment decisions. As billionaire investor Warren Buffett notes, "Only when you combine sound intellect with emotional discipline do you get rational behavior."

A direct link exists between emotions and investing behavior. *Emotional finance* addresses the key role emotions play in financial activities exploring the role of unconscious processes as they relate to financial decision-making. Such processes not only affect actions of individual investors, but also can influence overall market behavior. Positive emotions can lead to optimism, and optimism can lead to a greater willingness to take risk. Conversely, negative emotions can lead to pessimism that can depress the willingness to take risk.

Do emotions enhance or hurt decision-making? In the case of investment decision-making, the increased willingness to take risk based on positive emotions could lead to excessive risk-taking. Yet positive emotions also provide the impetus to act. Conversely, negative emotions can result in paralysis and inaction resulting from a decreased willingness to assume risk, which can also be a product of previous bad experiences in investing. People use various unconscious defenses to guard against the emotional pain of having to acknowledge that what they thought was an excellent investment has fallen short of expectations. On a broader scale, emotions can also help explain asset pricing bubbles, crashes, and related market phenomena.

How Do Emotional Biases Differ from Cognitive Biases?

Emotional biases involve emotions or feelings and cognitive biases associated with conscious thoughts. Given that cognition and emotion jointly drive all financial decisions, they have a complementary role to play in understanding investor activity and market behavior. Although the effects of cognitive and emotional biases are similar, finding a solution to emotional biases often requires greater care because these biases are ingrained in a person's psyche. Cognitive errors are based on faulty reasoning, a lack of understanding techniques related to analyzing investments, the inability to correctly process information, or memory errors. Common emotional biases are loss-aversion bias, overconfidence bias, self-control bias, status quo bias, endowment bias, and regret-aversion bias.

What Is Loss-Aversion Bias and How Does It Affect Decision-Making?

Have you ever felt a reluctance to sell an asset for less than what you paid for it? Maybe you hoped that if you held on long enough, its value would increase and you could at least break even. Have you ever wanted to lock in a profit on an asset as quickly as possible for fear that it may not last? If so, you probably suffer from *loss-aversion bias*, which is a tendency to feel more pain from a loss than pleasure from an equal gain. Loss aversion is associated with the *disposition effect* of holding onto losers too long and selling winners too quickly. Investors subject to loss-aversion bias think in terms of gains and losses, not risk and expected return. In the world of behavioral finance, most investors mentally and emotionally assess their current financial situation based on a beginning or reference point. A *reference point* is a benchmark that you already know, which helps you understand or make a judgment about another situation. Reference dependence is a fundamental principle of prospect theory. For example, an investor suffering from loss aversion would be more inclined to sell a security priced at $50 if she paid $40 for it (a reference point) than if she paid $60.

Mitigating loss aversion requires focusing less on whether the investment is currently facing a gain or a loss and more on the prospects for the security going forward. Such a strategy means relying on fundamental analysis and expectations of the asset's future value, rather than focusing on its past performance. *Fundamental analysis* is a method that attempts to measure the actual value of a company or an asset by examining related economic, financial, and other qualitative and quantitative factors. Another approach in dealing with loss-aversion bias is to ask whether you would buy this investment today if you didn't already own it. If your answer is no, then why are you still holding it? Gaining this awareness can help motivate you to sell a losing investment and buy one with better prospects. In short, as an investor, you need to be able to cope with the mental anguish of recognizing losses.

What Is Overconfidence Bias and What Potential Pitfalls Are Associated with It?

Assume someone asked you to evaluate your abilities as a driver compared to other drivers. If you are like most people, you will likely rank yourself above average, perhaps even among the best. Not every driver is above average. Likewise, not everyone who invests is as good as he or she might think. In investing, *overconfidence bias* is when market participants overestimate their intuitive ability or reasoning skills when investing. It is a type of self-deception bias. Overconfident investors become victims of their own ego and fall into the "superiority trap."[1]

Various factors lead to overconfidence bias. For instance, overconfidence is often associated with an unconscious desire to impress others by projecting a positive self-image. Overconfident investors can exhibit this trait by speaking more confidently about skills and talents than their records might otherwise support. Another factor that leads to overconfidence is an *illusion of knowledge*, which describes the tendency of people to think they know more than they really do. For example, many drivers who say they know how a car works really don't. For investors, this illusion may manifest itself by focusing on big wins in the past and neglecting investments that underperformed. The illusion of knowledge may also be associated with where investors went to school or the companies for which they have worked.

As a result of overconfidence, investors are likely to underestimate risk and overestimate return. Their underestimation of risk stems from the fact that they view their estimates of performance to be less susceptible to risk than the asset actually warrants. Because overconfident investors consider their selection skills to be superior, they overestimate the return potential for their selections. Thinking they are better than they really are at selecting securities, overconfident investors are less likely to see the value in portfolio diversification, perhaps thinking that such an exercise only dilutes the performance of their top selections. This behavior leads to underdiversification and suboptimal decisions. Because overconfident investors are quick to identify the next big winner, they often engage in excessive turnover of their portfolios, leading to higher transaction costs, which further lower their returns.

If you are an overconfident investor, you can mitigate this bias by maintaining detailed records of investment decisions such as trades, including the motivation associated with each decision. By doing so, you should be able to take a more balanced view of your track record. Overconfident investors should also keep track of their investment performance relative to the strategy pursued. Investigating successes and failures relative to the strategy allows for a more objective analysis of whether your performance is tied to skill or luck. The latter is evidenced by market forces.

What Role Does Overconfidence Play in Financial Decision-Making, Especially Relating to Investment Failure and Possible Errors in Investor Decisions?

Overconfidence bias occurs when market participants overestimate their own ability to do well in trading and investing. Much evidence shows a connection between overconfident investors and investment failures. For example, overconfident investors tend to trade more frequently, which leads to inferior cost-adjusted performance.[2] Overconfidence is associated with males more than females. Men tend to trade more actively than women, with corresponding inferior performance. According to one study, men trade 45% more often than women and consequently experience lower returns.[3]

Day traders are often overconfident investors due to the frequency of their trading. *Day trading* is the activity of buying and selling financial instruments with the intent of profiting from price movements in the underlying security within a single trading day. One study reports that day traders underperform, with only 20% of them earning positive net returns in any given year and less than 1% doing so in two consecutive years.[4] Hence, being a day trader can be bad for your wealth.

What Is Self-Control Bias and How Can It Affect Investment Performance?

Have you ever established fitness- or health-related goals as New Year's resolutions, only to meet failure as your exercise routine stops or you indulge in foods you wanted to avoid? Similar behavior can be observed among people who establish long-term financial goals, such as saving for their children's education or their own retirement. Their intentions are good, but short-term distractions easily divert the funds earmarked for a longer-term goal. This behavior is called *self-control bias* and is characterized by a lack of self-discipline, favoring immediate gratification over long-term goals. As a result, people replace their longer-term goals with more modest ones, a process known as *satisficing*.

Self-control bias can lead to ineffective investment behavior. Investors suffering from this bias often neglect longer-term goals to satisfy their short-term desires. They may fail to adequately prepare for retirement and delay it because they can't meet their spending needs, or they compromise their standard of living in retirement. Focusing on the short term also leads to asset allocation imbalances, with investors maintaining excess liquidity in case they decide to make a purchase on a whim.

What can you do to lessen self-control bias? Mitigating it requires establishing short-, medium-, and long-term goals as part of a broader investment strategy. Accomplishing each set of goals requires investors suffering from self-control bias to maintain an appropriate asset allocation. Establishing and sticking to a budget can also help prevent overconsumption.

What Is Status Quo Bias and Why Do Investors Fall Victim to It?

Do you have a retirement investment plan? One such plan is a *defined contribution plan*, in which both the employer and the employee provide funds for the employee to invest for retirement. In this arrangement, the employee makes all the decisions about how to invest the money and thus bears the risk for the decisions made. With the proliferation of options available, many employees seek advice from workshops the company provides or from trusted friends or family. Once they make an initial allocation, many individuals are reluctant to make changes or believe that the investment process is complete. This example illustrates *status quo bias*, which is a preference for things to stay the same. People therefore do nothing, sticking with a decision made previously.[5] In other words, these individuals continue with their original decisions out of inertia. Their comfort with the existing allocation leads to an unwillingness to make changes. If their original allocation occurred immediately before a bull market, not rebalancing the portfolio can result in a portfolio that is too risky, as equity allocations can shift substantially upward in a rising market. Circumstances and needs shift over time. What was an appropriate asset allocation at age 25 is probably inappropriate at 60. Without making changes, people may hold portfolios with inappropriate levels of risk, leaving an overconcentration in a particular asset class. In some cases, they have an overconcentration in their own employer's stock. A bias against change may keep investors from considering more appropriate investments.

Status quo bias is particularly hard to mitigate, as many people live by the motto "If it ain't broke, don't fix it." Investors suffering from this bias require education to better understand the trade-offs between risk and expected return and the importance of proper asset allocation. You need to be aware that asset allocation should shift over time to ensure you accomplish your goals as time horizons become shorter.

What Is Endowment Bias as Related to Investors?

Have you ever inherited something, such as shares of stock, that you refuse to sell even though it is inappropriate for your risk tolerance or does little for your portfolio's diversification? If so, you may suffer from endowment bias. *Endowment bias* occurs when investors hold onto or overvalue an asset because it is "special" simply because they own it. Thus, they feel it is more valuable than others consider it to be. Stated differently, your willingness to pay for an asset that is identical to one you hold is less than what you are willing to accept to sell. For example, how much would you be willing to pay for NCAA Final Four basketball tickets? If you already had the tickets, at what price would you be willing to sell them? Experiments show that people demand 14 times more money to sell tickets they hold than they would be willing to pay to buy them.[6]

Mitigating the endowment effect requires openly exploring whether the assets you hold are appropriate for your investment strategy. This includes investigating the role of each asset to evaluate whether owning it now makes sense. Researching the risk-return performance of the assets you hold and comparing them to similar assets you don't hold is likely to provide a more objective analysis. You should consider replacing familiar assets that are counterproductive to achieving your goals.

What Is Regret-Aversion Bias and How Can It Affect Investors?

Have you ever sold a stock and then watched it double in price? Have you ever considered selling a stock, decided to keep it, and then watched its price plummet? How did you feel? You probably felt the mentally uncomfortable pain of regret. People naturally want to avoid this feeling.

These following examples are two forms of regret: the regret of commission and the regret of omission. The *regret of commission* is the regret felt after acting, such as selling a stock that doubled—you wished you hadn't acted. The *regret of omission* is the regret felt after failing to act, such as not selling a stock that plummeted—you wished you had done something. The regret of commission is much stronger. That is, you feel more pain after an action turns out badly. You want to avoid regret, especially the regret of commission. When someone is in doubt, avoiding the regret of commission leads to doing nothing. However, you can take this avoidance too far and let it affect your ability to make good decisions. When this behavior occurs, it is called regret-aversion bias.

Regret-aversion bias leads to failure to take action out of fear of being wrong. Such a mentality leads to excess conservatism, resulting in avoiding riskier assets, which have a higher likelihood of declining in value. Regret-aversion bias can lead to long-term underperformance that can jeopardize goals. Herding behavior, an example of regret-aversion bias, happens when people take action that goes with the consensus or popular opinion. Such behavior reduces the blame investors feel because, after all, many others thought the same way.

Education is the primary mitigation tool. Rather than reacting to gains and losses, you need to better understand the concepts of risk and expected return. Such an approach helps to ensure that investment performance becomes less personal and more objective.

How Can Emotions and Moods Affect Investment Decision-Making?

Have you ever made an impulse purchase based on emotions? Perhaps a captivating advertisement nudged you to buy the latest iPhone. The same type of behavior can occur in the financial markets. Emotions and moods differ. *Emotions* are a physical response to change that results from a known cause. By contrast, *moods* are less specific and intense but last longer than emotions and have no clear starting point. Emotions can cover a wide range, whereas moods are either positive or negative. In the aggregate, both emotions and moods can distort how stocks get priced in the financial markets, causing prices to escalate to unsustainable heights, then plunge based on some trigger event or change in market dynamics.

So how do emotions and moods affect investment decision-making? Some contend that emotions can enhance decision-making, as when primitive man would face an animal in the wild, activating a "fight or flight" response.[7] However, such emotion-based behavior can be inappropriate and detrimental. Technical analysis, for instance, often relies on the ability to discern patterns in financial charts, and an investor relying on emotion may see patterns where they don't actually exist. *Technical analysis* is a methodology used to forecast the direction of markets or prices of individual securities by studying the past price and volume data. Thus, emotions may detract from portfolio success, resulting in inferior financial performance. Clearly, emotions affect investors' behavior in financial markets and the resulting effects on pricing.

Research on emotions finds an association between occurrences unrelated to the financial markets, such as phases of the moon, sporting events, cinema films, and market behavior. In fact, emotion can affect the performance of an entire stock market. Studies have linked international sporting events to increases in stock market valuations, despite no changes in market fundamentals.[8]

How Can Emotions and Moods Affect Markets?

Emotion can affect the manner in which people react to news in both the short and long term. In the short run, investors tend to react slowly (underreact) to new information in the market but exhibit too much faith in longer-term patterns, resulting in overreaction. If such patterns continue, emotions can fuel financial market bubbles and crashes that have been attributed to market instability, dating back to the 1630s with the tulip mania.

With the advent of a formal futures market in Holland, tulip bulbs served as the basis for a mania in which a single tulip bulb sold for more than 10 times the annual income of a skilled craftsman. A *futures market* is a central financial exchange in which people can enter into a contract to buy specific quantities of a commodity or financial instrument at a specified price with delivery at a specified future date. People became increasingly interested in tulip bulbs as more individuals began buying bulbs at increasing prices with the intention of reselling, despite the outrageous pricing structure that emerged. Ultimately, in early 1637, the market bubble burst, and prices plummeted as traders panicked in fear of losing money.[9]

Tulip mania relates to what is known as the emotional finance framework, which is based on the work of Freud,[10] which produces the potential for emotional "roller-coasters" in terms of market reactions. The process develops as some initial mysterious, magical innovation, such as the tulip market, or more recently dot-com-based stock or failure of the subprime mortgage securities that contributed to the financial crisis of 2007–2008, draws the attention of the investing public.

Here is the process by which a market bubble develops and then bursts. Initially, investors view such investments as infallible, with the likelihood of success near certainty. Next, they create separate buckets in which they split investor risk ("the pain") from the excitement associated with the innovation ("the pleasure"). The pain associated with risk becomes a part of the unconscious mind. Investors focusing on the excitement of the investments in the conscious mind begin to value the innovations based on their excitement capacity, beyond their potential for financial rewards. Furthermore, they hold any positive views by experts, such as financial analysts, academics, and the press, about their investment decisions in the highest regard. What results is a mass buying of the innovation, creating an irrational bubble. Investors become willing to pay irrationally high prices that greatly exceed the fundamental values of such investments. Ultimately a tipping point arrives, prompted by nagging doubts. At this point, investors are flooded with strong distaste for the innovation on a conscious level, resulting in a dismissal of those they previously viewed as experts. At this stage, investors blame the experts for their actions. As more and more investors assume this view, widespread panic emerges and a massive sell-off occurs. Thus, the bubble bursts and the market crashes.[11]

Another example of a reliance on longer-term patterns is the technology bubble that occurred between 1995 and 2000. Investors began to see the ever-increasing values of technology stocks as sustainable despite fundamental measures that indicated otherwise. Thus, emotional responses may cause market prices to diverge from true values, and under- or overvaluation resulting from reactions to news in the short or long run. For example, in the 18 months leading up to early March 2000, the Dow Jones Internet Index multiplied six times. During March and early April 2000, the index fell by 50% and by the end of 2002 stood at only 8% of its high.[12]

How Are Emotions Mitigated or Magnified When Making Investment Decisions?

Do you sometimes make decisions based on your emotional state at the time? Do emotionally based decisions enhance or detract from investment performance? Considerable debate exists about how emotions affect investor decision-making. Some contend that investors take excessive risk when in a positive mood. In contrast, investor anxiety may result in paralysis, inaction, and insufficient risk-taking.[13]

Emotions and moods may affect both investor decision-making and the financial markets. For example, emotions and moods can lead investors to react to events unrelated to the companies in which they trade stocks. Company announcements can lead to emotionally based over- or underreaction to news, causing inefficient herding behavior in the financial markets. Despite this debate, the overall evidence suggests that, on balance, emotions hinder investors in making effective decisions.

Mitigating emotional biases is more challenging than countering cognitive biases. Although you can often lessen cognitive biases through education and through alterations in your decision-making process, emotional biases tend to be associated with your psychological makeup and can be influenced by changes in mood.

What Are Cultural Biases?

How does culture affect various economic outcomes? Does your ethnicity, religion, race, or family history affect how you view economic decisions and, in turn, your investment decisions? Research shows that culture has a direct impact on expectations and preferences, which in turn affect economic outcomes. How our ancestors operated provides a basis for an inherited culture, which affects the way people view the world. This causal relation emerges through trust. Trust affects the willingness to exchange financial assets. For example, some people are more trustful than others based on the culture in which they reside. Thus, cultural standards and proximity also affect behavior among individual investors.[14] For example, investors are more likely to own stocks in firms that communicate in the investor's native tongue and that have a chief executive of the same cultural background. Investors are also more inclined to hold investments in companies located in close proximity to them. The effects are strongest for less savvy investment institutions and individual investors.[15]

Various name-induced stereotypes affect investor preferences for managers. For instance, investors tend to allocate less money to an index fund operated by managers with foreign-sounding names. These funds have a greater decline in fund flow after a period of bad market performance than do other funds operated by those who have non-foreign-sounding names. *Fund flow* refers to the net of all cash inflows and outflows in and out of a financial asset. International events can also alter investing patterns. For instance, after the September 11, 2001, terrorist attacks in the United States, fund flows to funds operated by managers having Middle Eastern–sounding names declined markedly.[16]

How Do Trust and Home Bias Influence
Financial Decision-Making?

Having addressed the link between culture and economic outcomes, let's now turn to the subject of how culture affects financial decision-making. Evidence shows that culture influences economic behavior, such as saving and investment decisions, market participation rates, and cross-border investment and trade. A history of conflicts between countries, religious differences, and even genetics play a role in investing patterns within and across countries. These differences influence trust, which affects economic exchange and ultimately investment patterns.[17] Investment patterns should be explored from the perspective of both individuals and institutions, such as endowments, pension plans, life insurance companies, and banks. Culture influences the behavior of institutional investors, which in turn influences individual investors.

Behavioral-based investor preferences often exhibit a *home bias* toward what is comfortable to them culturally and geographically. Investors are generally drawn to companies that are located close to them, communicate in the same language, and have chief executives from similar cultural backgrounds. Although both individual and institutional investors tend to behave in the same manner, this home bias toward culturally similar firms is greater for individual investors.[18]

How Does Social Interaction Influence
People, Especially When Investing?

Culture is an important determinant on how individuals view economic outcomes. Beyond culture, what other social factors have a role in influencing investor decisions? Does the manner in which your parents or friends approach investing influence you? Clearly, various social factors contribute to how people approach investment. Such factors include social interaction, social identity, social norms, and social capital. An investor's network, which includes family, friends, coworkers, and neighbors, influences these social factors. Although each group has the potential to play an important role in defining investment behavior, the family typically has the strongest impact. In fact, investors' likelihood of entering the stock market within the next five years is 20% to 30% higher if their parents or children entered the stock market during the past five years. This finding persists despite the physical distance between family members. Today's means of communicating with those who are distant actually seem to have minimized the role proximity played in the influence that neighbors, fellow churchgoers, and colleagues had in the past.[19]

What Social Role Do Investment Clubs Play in Investing?

Have you ever participated in an investment club? Investment clubs are typically set up so that members can pool their money for the purpose of sharing responsibility for stock selection and providing diversification for members. Group dynamics is a specific source of social interaction that occurs in this type of setting. One might assume that the collective wisdom of the members fosters an environment in which superior performance would be expected. However, emotional biases can be rampant, as investors often exhibit loss aversion because recognizing a loss is a loss for the member who advocated buying the security. Thus, members who recommended a losing stock tend to advocate holding onto it despite a lack of evidence for a turnaround. In fact, one study finds that investment clubs underperform the market even more than individual investors do. This finding supports the conclusion that while investment clubs encourage savings, promote education about financial markets, and increase social ties, they don't produce superior returns.[20]

Furthermore, both investment clubs and individual investors are more likely to invest in a stock that has a good image. For instance, a company might be on a most-admired companies list. Groups favor such stocks more than individual investors do even though such laurels may not indicate strong performance. Investment clubs tend to select admired companies because members need reasons to support their selections. Thus, the quality of a reason outweighs the more complex cost-benefit analysis that could produce more balanced outcomes.[21]

How Do Social Identity and Social Norms Influence People, Especially When Investing?

Beyond social interaction, social identity and social norms can play a critical role in influencing the decision-making of investors. An individual's social identity or personal sense of self affects investment behavior. Investor identity is associated with different social categories and thus predicts how someone in a particular category is likely to behave. Specific examples of social identity are a person's civic engagement and political orientation. Identity helps to explain types of behavior that may be detrimental. One person's actions can influence another's actions within a category of social identity. Identity can also reveal how preferences can change. These changed preferences can emerge from advertising campaigns or from actual changing of social categories. Finally, people have the potential to choose whom they want to be, and such decisions are often associated with behaviors exhibited by the chosen group.[22]

Politically active individuals, regardless of their political affiliation, are more likely to be exposed to financial news. In fact, those who are politically active are much more likely to participate in the stock market. In general, politically more active individuals spend about 30 minutes more on news daily and are more knowledgeable about the economy and the markets as a result.[23] Where someone falls on the political spectrum also affects that individual's likelihood of investing in the stock market. Moderate left voters are less likely to invest in stocks than are moderate right voters. Such a finding is consistent with the notion that personal values affect invest-ment decisions, leading to "stock market aversion" among political subgroups.[24] Individual investors perceive stock mar-kets as less risky and more undervalued when their own party is in power. In fact, investors increase the proportion of risky assets in their portfolios when the political climate aligns with their views.[25]

How Does Social Capital Influence People, Especially When Investing?

Social capital created by trust also influences investment re-turns. In general, *social capital* refers to connections with other people and can be measured by the general lifestyles in a community that promote social and political engagements. Changes in work, family structure, age, level of suburban life, media, and gender roles also affect social capital.[26] *Trust* refers to the confidence of receiving fair returns in economic transac-tions. Stock market participation appears to be directly related to the trust exhibited by investors in society. Beyond helping community development, higher social capital for communi-ties leads to better financial development, including a higher share in stocks among liquid assets.[27]

Where a lack of trust exists, stock market participation is lower.[28] In addition to trust, stock market literacy explains the probability of participation. The share of investment in stocks is then conditional on participation. A link also exists between financial literacy and trust levels.[29] Trust influences investment risk perceptions and is directly related to affect. In this context, *affect* is the positive or negative feeling associated with a par-ticular investment choice.[30]

Trust can also be associated with corporate policies, such as dividend policy. For example, less trusting individuals tend to prefer dividend-paying, as opposed to non-dividend-paying, stocks. In fact, in countries and in regions in the United States in which people exhibit less trust, investors assign locally headquartered firms that pay dividends higher value than those that are not locally headquartered and don't pay dividends.[31]

The behaviors of individual investors respond to changes in trust. For example, stock market participation typically declines in a state after revelation of a prominent corporate fraud case in that state. Individuals decrease their holdings in nonfraudulent firms located in that state even if they did not hold stock in the fraudulent firm. Households with more experience with corporate fraud tend to hold less equity.[32]

Large-scale scandals take their toll on trust and impact investing patterns. For instance, Bernie Madoff's Ponzi scheme resulted in a reduction of brokerage accounts and an increase in savings accounts for residents of communities that were relatively more exposed to fraud. A *Ponzi scheme* is an investing scam that promises high rates of return with little risk to investors. In a Ponzi scheme, the scammer uses funds from new investors to pay the earlier backers.

How Does Attitude Affect Investment Decision-Making?

Your attitude can influence your decision-making. In fact, Warren Buffett once remarked that "the most important quality for an investor is temperament, not intellect." Let's return to the notion of regret-aversion bias, which relates to one's attitude. Regret-aversion bias can sway investors to prefer to keep what they have and do nothing in order to avoid potential blame associated with making a change. Investors want to avoid the feelings of regret associated with a bad investment choice, but how do feelings affect investors at the time of decision-making? Have you, for instance, made a financial decision at a time when you were unhappy? Would you have made the same decision had you been in a better mood? Mood and emotion, the states of feelings at the time of decision-making, may influence investor behavior.

Investors react to risk at two major levels. On a cognitive level, they attempt to assess probabilities and outcomes. On an emotional level, many investors face risk with fear, even if they understand the nature of their fear. Divergent thoughts can emerge as investors are torn between the fear associated with risk and the cognitive evaluation of the threat posed by the risk.[33]

Neuroeconomics is the study of the relation between the parts of the brain generating emotional states and how the brain processes information about risk, rewards, and punishments. Positive emotions lead to optimism and an increased willingness to take risk as investors grow more confident in their ability to analyze investment options. By contrast, anxiety and other negative emotions reduce investor confidence. Outcomes of past choices that alter how they view similar future financial decisions often influence investors.[34]

Moods and emotions can be based on internal programming and past experiences, but can also be influenced by outside stimuli, including sports events. For example, the negative mood associated with elimination from the World Cup can result in a negative abnormal stock return in the country that lost the match. International cricket, rugby, and basketball games produce similar results.[35] Likewise, national disasters can affect mood, which in turn affects stock market returns. For example, aviation disasters can lead to a negative mood, depressing stock market returns.

Recurring and predictable events can also affect mood. Likewise, cultural, religious, and celebratory holidays can influence stock market performance. Research indicates that St. Patrick's Day and Rosh Hashanah both produce enhanced stock market performance, as mood is elevated and lead to greater investor confidence and lower risk aversion. Some holidays differentially influence individual stock performance, based on the proportion of people who celebrate the holiday and the nature of the company.[36] Likewise, stock returns are significantly higher with lower volatility during Ramadan for

14 primarily Muslim countries. The results imply that feelings of solidarity and social identity lead to optimistic beliefs, which in turn positively influence investment performance.[37]

Do Weather Conditions Influence Investor Decisions?

Does the amount of sunshine affect your decision-making? Do adverse weather conditions influence your mood? Does the number of hours of daylight drive investor behavior? The answers to these questions is generally yes. *Seasonal affective disorder* (SAD) is a condition that affects many individuals during seasons of fewer daylight hours or in geographical locations with fewer days of sunshine. SAD has been linked not only with depression but also with lower risk-taking behavior. Research indicates that a direct link exists between SAD and inferior stock market performance, particularly in northern countries.[38]

Let's look at some other situations in which weather conditions can influence investor behavior. One study explored the relation between morning sunshine in the city of a country's leading stock exchange and the daily returns of that exchange. The results show that sunshine is correlated with stock returns.[39] In another study, sunniness has a positive effect on the demand for stocks, and a full moon has a negative effect. Precipitation and daylight saving are both negatively related to stock demand.[40]

What Measures Are Available for Gauging Investor Sentiment and Why Is Measuring Investor Sentiment Important?

Investor sentiment refers to collective beliefs, preferences, and attitudes that reflect investors' affective state. Both sentiment and mood measure the level of collective optimism of investors about market states and asset values. Mood differs from sentiment in that mood is tied to emotions that can change frequently (e.g., daily), but sentiment is tied to attitudes that are relatively slow to change.[41]

Investor sentiment can also be interpreted as the propensity to speculate. More specifically, *market-wide sentiment* is the difference between the beliefs of sentiment-driven traders and an asset's true or intrinsic value. Such noise trading can lead to a large divergence between market prices and fundamental values. *Noise trading* is a term used to describe an investor who decides to buy or sell without using fundamental data. Various financial market anomalies can be explained by the idea of noise trader risk, including excess volatility of, and mean reversion, in stock market prices, as well as the undervaluation of closed-end mutual funds.[42]

Interestingly, various indices attempt to measure mood. Facebook's Gross National Happiness (GNH) index is calculated using the textual analysis of emotion words posted by users on Facebook. An increase in the volatility of GNH results in an increase in the next day's stock market returns. Investors can also use the GNH to predict future trading volume.[43] One study used daily internet search volume from millions of households to reveal market-level sentiment. The authors aggregated the volume of queries related to household concerns including "recession," "unemployment," and "bankruptcy." Using these queries, they constructed a Financial and Economic Attitudes Revealed by Search (FEARS) index to measure investor sentiment. Increases in FEARS lead to return reversals. That is, a high FEARS index is associated with low returns today, but high returns occur over the following two days.[44]

Not only does investor sentiment affect the stock market, but the stock market also seems to influence investor sentiment. Studying a sample spanning roughly three decades, researchers found that daily fluctuations in stock prices have an almost immediate impact on the physical health of investors, with a sharp price decline increasing hospitalization rates over the next two days. The effect is particularly strong for conditions related to mental health, such as anxiety, suggesting that concerns over shocks to both current and future consumption influence investors' perception of their well-being.[45]

4

INVESTOR BEHAVIOR

How investors behave can affect both their portfolio performance and the overall market. Because of a lack of formal training, limited experience, or personality traits, investors don't always make decisions that are consistent with their stated financial goals. Their decisions often are impulsive and at odds with rational decision-making. Such decisions can cause them to trade too frequently, which increases trading costs and can increase tax obligations. Those engaged in excessive trading often forget about the importance of holding a diversified portfolio. They have forgotten the expression "Don't put all of your eggs in one basket." This piece of advice means that someone should not concentrate all efforts and resources in one area because doing so could result in losing everything. When applied to investing, putting your eggs in one basket is the equivalent of putting all of your savings into one asset, such as a stock, mutual fund, or real property. Thus, such investors may take on unnecessary risk due to a lack of proper diversification. Additionally, peer groups or demographic characteristics, such as gender, education level, or race, may influence how investors make decisions. These behaviors are not limited to individual investors. Professional investors can also fall prey to behaviors that lead them and their clients to inferior outcomes. This chapter addresses common types of investor behavior and how it influences decision-making and performance.

How Can Behavioral Biases Affect Investment Performance?

Behavioral biases can negatively affect your investment performance. Some behavioral biases cause investors to sell superior investments out of fear of losing a gain, while holding onto inferior ones to avoid having to recognize a loss. If you've ever gone to a casino, you may have found yourself wanting to cash out a gain because you feared you might lose it. Or conversely, you may have kept gambling in hopes that you could recover your losses. The same concept applies to how people view their investments. This type of decision-making framework is known as *loss aversion*. Focusing on gains and losses instead of an investment's prospects can produce subpar investment performance and potential tax effects. Although most countries don't tax individuals on increases in the value of investments they continue to hold, taxable events are triggered when they sell an investment, such as a stock, at a gain. The tax rates are often higher when the recognized gain occurs within a short time horizon, such as a year or less.

Frequent and even excessive trading is sometimes associated with investors exhibiting overconfidence in their decision-making. Overconfident investors often don't pursue adequate portfolio diversification, exposing themselves to higher levels of risk. Often these same investors believe they are really good at investing and thus prefer to select a few stocks and watch them closely rather than to hold diversified portfolios. Just like keeping your eggs in different baskets, you can diversify away some of the risk of holding stock in any individual company by having the stocks of many companies in a portfolio. But overconfident investors take more risk than needed and usually don't achieve returns that compensate them for the risk assumed.

People view risk in different ways. Some enjoy risky bets, while others shy away from taking them. The degree of an investor's reluctance to take risks and to prefer less risky alternatives is known as *risk aversion*. A person's level of risk

aversion can change based on overall stock market movements and individual investing experiences. For example, investors tend to become more risk-averse after watching the
stock market decline. Down or bear markets cause them to reduce their allocation to stocks. Conversely, after an extended
bull market, investor risk aversion decreases, and they tend
to hold a greater proportion of their portfolio in stocks. A *bull
market* is one in which stock prices trend upward for an extended period. In a *bear market* securities prices fall, and widespread pessimism causes the stock market's downward spiral
to be self-sustaining. The implication of such actions results
in individual investors typically doing a poor job at market
timing because they sell stocks at the bottom of a cycle and buy
them at the top. Buying high and selling low is a disastrous
strategy. Warren Buffett addresses this behavior by encour-
aging investors to go against their natural biases: "Investors
should remember that excitement and expenses are their enemies. And if they insist on trying to time their participation in
equities, they should try to be fearful when others are greedy
and greedy only when others are fearful."[1]

Recall that a cognitive bias is sometimes associated with
heuristics. *Heuristics* are simple, efficient rules that people use
to increase the speed of decisions and judgments. By using
heuristics, people limit the amount of information they use to
make decisions. Investors who experience cognitive biases may
select suboptimal portfolios because they lack the information
that would allow them to explore a wider range of investment
options. As a result, cognitive biases affect investment choices,
which in turn may influence portfolio performance.

Cognitive biases also result from faulty cognitive reasoning
or the inability to process information necessary to analyze investment options. Such limitations can cause investors to over-
simplify decision-making by taking shortcuts. A lack of retention
of key information necessary to make educated investment decisions can diminish portfolio performance. Many investors
suffering from cognitive biases struggle to incorporate in their

analysis such statistical principles as *correlation*, the manner in which asset prices change with respect to each other. Correlation can take on values between −1 and +1. If two securities have a high positive correlation, a value close to +1, they tend to experience similar return patterns. Although they are distinct securities, you have two securities that behave in a similar way, a tendency to keep in mind if you want to diversify your portfolio. A value of zero means no relation exists between the securities, and a value of −1 means they move in opposite directions.

Left unchecked, investors experiencing cognitive biases may cling to their original set of experiences, which is referred to as *belief perseverance*. Efforts to reduce cognitive biases through training and education are often successful, certainly more successful than mitigating emotional biases, which stem from one's psychological makeup. The best mitigation efforts directly target the bias through education and experience, which leads to higher levels of sophistication.

How Do Overconfidence and Self-Attribution Affect Investor Decision-Making?

Most people view their own abilities in a positive light, erring on the side of a more favorable assessment than their track record deserves. For example, people tend to rate their driving abilities better than average. Yet most people can't be above average. How many individuals would assess their physical appearance as average? Everyday examples of overconfidence help us understand why investors become overconfident. Because of selected recall or an inflated ego, investors often think of their stock picking and timing skills as superior. Yet most individual investors trade in the wrong direction and at the wrong time. Even professional investors, who have the tools, resources, and experience that most individuals lack, still have difficulty outperforming the market.

One of the more common factors that affect investors' decision-making is overconfidence, especially when coupled with self-attribution bias. *Self-attribution* is associated with taking personal credit for past successes while blaming other factors for failures. Pushed by self-attribution, overconfident investors put too much emphasis on their own views in decision-making and too little emphasis on public information and the views of others. George Soros, a highly successful investor, helps to keep self-attribution biases in check by keeping a journal log of the reasoning behind his every investment decision. Analyzing this log helps him differentiate between results that come from skill and those that come from luck.

When many investors exhibit the same behavior, their combined influence can affect the overall market, as illustrated by the run-up of technology stock prices in the 1990s and real estate in the 2000s. *Momentum strategies* occur when asset price trajectories continue for an extended period, sometimes as long as two years, without subsequent news that supports the movement. Affected investors get caught up in the euphoria of an emerging trend and join the crowd to avoid missing out. This phenomenon, called *herding behavior*, is a type of social bias. Wiser heads typically prevail at some point when market analytics show that a security or the overall market is overvalued. Thus, overconfidence leads not only to overtrading, but also to errors in assessment due to investors' overestimation of whatever stock information they possess.

Two common stock anomalies attributed to overconfidence are value and size. An *anomaly* arises when opportunities exist repeatedly to earn returns not explained by financial theories. Value anomalies occur when the market is too punitive on a company experiencing bad news or as investors overreact to prospects for growth stocks, leaving value stocks undervalued. A *value stock* is one in which the stock price trades below what would otherwise be expected based on objective measures of performance, such as its earnings or sales. Thus, the term *value* suggests that an investor is buying stock that is relatively less expensive. In contrast, a *growth stock* is one in which market participants have bid up its price to an excessively high level, overpaying for the successful financial metrics of performance. Once again, this overreaction is often mitigated by wiser heads, as value stocks typically outperform growth stocks over longer time periods.[2]

The size anomaly occurs when, even after adjusting for differential risk factors, smaller-cap firms tend to outperform larger companies over extended periods. The term *cap* is an abbreviation of *capitalization*. *Market capitalization* refers to the total dollar market value of a company's outstanding shares, determined by multiplying its stock price by the number of outstanding shares.[3] The larger the cap, the larger the company.

How Do the Disposition Effect, Prospect Theory, and Sentiment Influence Investors' Behavior?

If you are an investor, do you tend to sell assets that have risen in price rather than sell those that have fallen in price? If so, you are guilty of the *disposition effect*. The disposition effect occurs as investors are attracted to riskier behavior and are willing to take a gamble in order to avoid recognizing a loss. Conversely, they tend to be repelled by risks when stocks are doing well, as they anxiously seek to lock in gains. The disposition effect is often a consequence of momentum. Price momentum causes a gap between a stock's intrinsic value and its price. Investors influenced by the disposition effect may not process new information correctly because they get caught up in the current stock price trend.

Prospect theory describes investors' tendency to evaluate outcomes according to gains and losses relative to a *reference point*, typically the purchase price, rather than based on risk and expected return. According to prospect theory, investors are inconsistent in their levels of risk aversion, showing differences in the way they face gains versus losses. In particular, they exhibit traditional risk-averse behavior when evaluating gains but tend to be more risk-seeking when approaching potential losses. The logic behind this difference is that investors have difficulty accepting a realized loss, so they are willing to engage in risky behavior in order to salvage a "win" with a losing investment. Indeed, people tend to hold losing stock positions in hopes of gaining back the losses and breaking even. The desire to break even with a losing stock is quite strong. This behavior is referred to as *loss aversion*.

Still another explanatory phenomenon for pricing behavior is *market sentiment*, which refers to the feeling or tone of a market as revealed through the activity and price movement of the securities traded in that market. For instance, rising stock prices indicate a bullish market sentiment, while falling stock prices indicate a bearish market sentiment.

How Does Limited Attention Affect One's Investing Choices?

Another bias affecting investor decision-making is *limited attention*, which is the tendency of people to neglect important, comprehensive information in lieu of recent news. Investors only have so much attention to focus on investment options and must be judicious about the amount and types of information they collect in the decision-making process. One example of this bias is category thinking. *Category thinking* refers to the tendency for investors to focus on broader market and sector information, rather than information about individual companies. Company advertisements or promotional campaigns are often effective in influencing stock prices, as investors feel overwhelmed by the volume of information coming from financial news sources. One study shows that a stock price that is at a 52-week high affects the behavior of the firm and its investors and explains a large portion of the momentum anomaly. A company that promotes its stock as a great investment when it is trading at a 52-week high is an example of positive framing. *Framing theory* contends that the way in which a concept is presented affects the decision-making process of individuals.

Determining which pieces of investment data are important and relevant can be difficult. Given the proliferation of financial news available through both broadcast media and the internet, people are often overwhelmed with information, complicating their ability to differentiate various types of information. Legitimate information allows for more educated decisions, while speculation and conjecture can sidetrack investors. Categorizing information requires time, education, and experience. Because most investors lack formal training or the time to properly filter information, they often make decisions in suboptimal ways and trade on noise rather than information.

What information do investors value? People are drawn to past performance as a basis for picking mutual funds. Unfortunately, as discussed previously, past performance is often a poor indication of future performance. Indeed, the government forces mutual fund advertising to include a statement to that effect. But people still use past returns as a major source of information when choosing a fund. Additionally, focusing exclusively on returns ignores the cost structure of funds. The costs associated with mutual fund ownership can be substantial, including front-end loads and operating expenses.[4] A *front-end load* represents the upfront charge, usually a percentage of the initial investment in the fund. *Operating expenses* are annual charges that reduce the net returns investors receive. Novice investors tend to ignore such expenses. Well-educated investors should consider both returns and costs. But people have a limited amount of time, so limited attention to decision-making can result in biased and poor investments.

Attention-grabbing news also enters into the process of stock selection. In establishing selection criteria, people are more likely to buy stocks that grab their attention, including those experiencing unusually high trading volumes or extreme one-day returns.[5] When more people are trading a stock, other investors tend to pay attention to that stock, which in turn further increases trading volume. In fact, investors are more likely to buy attention-grabbing stocks regardless of the company. Such investors don't challenge the information presented, asking whether it is factual or comprehensive. They may not consider the possibility that information is presented out of context or that the company selects data to present itself in the best possible light. Likewise, firms may omit information that would enable a more comprehensive analysis but show the firm in a less favorable position.

Firm advertisements can also be misleading to the point of being classified as devious. For example, evidence suggests that firms substantially increase advertising spending before insider sales. That is, managers apparently want to foster demand for the stock, which makes selling their own shares easier. Given that most investors have limited time to absorb and process information, they become vulnerable to such manipulation. Managers take advantage of this limited attention by using advertisements to boost short-term stock prices. Unfortunately for new investors, the stock price may return to a period of lower returns after the insider sales and advertising are completed.[6]

Why Do Some Investors Trade Too Much?

Excessive trading can erode gross performance for investors. *Gross performance* represents the return generated for an investor before subtracting the costs. Trading activity results in transaction costs and heightened emotions. One reason for frequent trading is investor overconfidence. As previously defined, overconfidence occurs when investors believe that their abilities are better than average, leading them to believe they can outperform the market indexes.[7] Proving that overconfidence is associated with frequent trading is difficult because there is no objective framework in which to identify the characteristics of traders who are overconfident. One proxy used to measure overconfidence is gender. The logic is that men are more confident in the investment arena and thus trade more frequently than women. Empirically, women do trade less often than men, but the reason is unclear. Gender is not just connected to more frequent trading, but also to differences in risk tolerance, which makes assigning gender as a proxy potentially ambiguous.[8]

Other studies investigate whether aggressive behavior such as speeding is related to trading frequency. Using speeding as a proxy for risky behavior, one study finds a positive relation between the number of recent speeding tickets and the volume of stock trading by male investors. Based on this study, risky financial behavior and risky driving may be related.[9] Overconfident investors who enjoy sensation-seeking behavior also trade more frequently. Regardless of whether a definitive gender-based relation is associated with overtrading, investors need to be educated about the downsides of excessive trading.

Those unfamiliar with the principles of investing often think of investing as another form of gambling. Evidence exists to support that association. Investors who enjoy gambling trade twice as frequently as those who don't. Three motives emerge to support a relation between frequent trading activity and gambling. First, investing, like gambling, can be a source of entertainment, a relation that some call the recreation-leisure motive. Second, individuals who see investing as a form of gambling possess an aspirational motive in which they overestimate the chance of a large payoff. Third, trading provides novelty to relieve boredom, often cited as a reason people gamble. This final motive supports the notion that both gambling and investing are emotional responses for the creation of hobbies that provide entertainment.[10] Some cite day trading as the intersection of trading and gambling desires. *Day trading* is the frequent buying and selling of stocks, often on the same day. This process typically occurs online and is motivated by trying to take advantage of short-term price movements.

Gambling is a stimulation or sensation-seeking motive that has taking a risk as its goal, while day trading becomes a driver for the risk-taking motive that has the outcome of selecting among risky choices. Evidence indicates that a desire for stimulation drives day traders more than a desire to make money. In other words, they enjoy the thrill of investing more than achieving profits. More trading activity means more expense, both transaction fees and the time spent trading.[11] Some researchers consider young men as at more risk for this type of behavior than young women. Why? Men are more closely linked to stimulation-seeking motives and exhibit greater overconfidence. Some investors may see gambling and investing as substitutes for one another, implying that increased opportunities to participate in lotteries may reduce the desire to trade frequently.

What Is Hyperbolic Discounting and Why Is It Important?

Why do some merchants advertise "Buy now, pay later?" Why do some people carry large credit card debt at a high interest rate while investing for retirement at a lower rate of return? Why do many people fail to save for retirement? Why would someone prefer to receive $5 right now instead of $10 in a month? One answer lies with the daunting term hyperbolic discounting.

Hyperbolic discounting is the tendency to prefer a return sooner, even if it is smaller, than a return later. That is, people desire an immediate reward rather than a higher-value, delayed reward. Although hyperbolic discounting is a cognitive bias that defies logic and common sense, it is everywhere. Such behavior implies that impulsivity levels are higher when people focus on making decisions based on achieving short-term rewards. Alternative choices that result in a delay become less attractive than more near-term and inferior opportunities. Returning to a previous example, the reason so many people fail to save for retirement is that no immediate reward exists for saving for the future.

In the absence of hyperbolic discounting, an investor with a return expectation of 10% annually should be indifferent between having $100 now and $110 a year from now.

Likewise, the investor should also be indifferent between receiving $100 in a year and $110 in two years. This relation is referred to as *exponential discounting*. However, this economic theory does not reflect how investors actually make choices. In fact, investors' behavior is more associated with hyperbolic discounting, which indicates that an investor is more able to wait for returns when both payouts are in the future. In the scenario presented above, such behavior implies that an investor is more likely to wait two years for the $110 than wait one year for $100. Yet people are unwilling to wait the same length of time, one year, to receive $110 when they can get $100 today. Something about receiving money today trumps waiting for more money later.

Let's take a look at a nonfinancial example of hyperbolic discounting that involves starting a diet-and-exercise program. People who are overweight may have a desire to improve their health. They may develop an exercise regimen and go on a diet. However, in the short term, they may forgo healthy choices in favor of unhealthy meals, stating that they will follow a stricter diet in the future. That is, people often splurge before starting a diet. Likewise, they may defer their exercise program due to immediate distractions. Thus, a disconnect occurs between long-term desires and the current willingness to achieve better health, as short-term decisions become inconsistent with the heavily discounted future benefits of healthier living.

Why Do Investors Hold Underdiversified Portfolios?

Underdiversification can be bad for your financial health. Diversification means that the gains from certain sectors or assets can offset losses from others. Let's examine some reasons for such underdiversification. One possible explanation is that investors are overconfident in their selection abilities and don't see the need to diversify what they assume are excellent portfolio choices. Another possible reason is that investors gravitate to stocks associated with industries about which they are relatively knowledgeable or with which they are comfortable. Such logic exposes them to excessive risk because their portfolio holdings are too similar and subject to the same market forces.

Now let's get more technical and discuss why diversification matters. A portfolio's overall risk consists of market risk and company-specific risk. *Market risk* refers to that portion of a portfolio's risk which could cause investors to experience losses due to factors influencing the overall performance of the financial markets. This risk can't be eliminated or diversified away. *Company-specific risk* refers to the portion of a portfolio's risk that is tied to performance of individual stocks held by investors. In order to minimize the overall risk in the portfolio, investors need to have appropriate levels of diversification, meaning they should hold a wide representation of different types of stocks, both domestically and abroad, and other assets. Diversification reduces and potentially eliminates the company-specific risk.

However, many investors fail to fully diversify their portfolio. One reason is that they exhibit *home bias*, a tendency to hold their portfolio in domestic securities rather than what would be held based on worldwide market weights. For example, in the United States, institutional investors hold about 72% of their assets in domestic equities, almost double the U.S. share, which is about 40%, of the world portfolio. Historically, reasons existed for such an imbalance. Restrictions on the ability for foreign investors to own stock and a lack of investment vehicles limited access to foreign markets. However, increased international access, a proliferation of international trading securities, and the introduction of internet trading have changed the investing landscape.

So why does a disparity to fully diversify a portfolio still exist? Investors' behavior may explain the persistence of such gaps. Overconfident investors may not perceive the need to diversify because they trust their research skills. Likewise, *familiarity bias*, a concept closely related to home bias, suggests that people are uncomfortable investing in companies of which they have little day-to-day awareness. Thus, they may deem a large retailer that has many locations abroad and is headquartered in another country as less desirable because it doesn't provide a potential in-person shopping experience.

Some, however, advocate underdiversified portfolios. For example, multibillionaire investor Warren Buffett, the chief executive officer and chairman of Berkshire Hathaway, once stated, "Diversification is protection against ignorance. It makes little sense if you know what you are doing." According to Buffett, researching several industries in great depth and using that knowledge to profit from those industries is more lucrative than spreading a portfolio across a broad array of industries or assets. Although Buffett's statement may have merit for highly knowledgeable people who employ a team of analysts, it is unlikely to apply to the typical investor who lacks investment knowledge, experience, and time to devote to investing.

How Do Personality Traits Affect Investors' Behavior?

Differences in personality traits are at the heart of emotional biases exhibited by investors. Although some investors are very detail-focused in their analysis of investments, others focus on broader themes and big-picture concepts of analysis. Still others are likely to make decisions based on how they feel about a company or product. For some, investing is a social experience, and the conversations they hold may influence the stocks they buy or sell. Some investors make decisions in an orderly and systematic way, while others are more impulsive. Studying personality traits provides a better understanding of investors' behavior.

Various paradigms exist to capture personality characteristics. One example is the Five-Factor Model of personality traits developed by Robert R. McCrae, a personality psychologist at the National Institute of Aging.[12] This model captures five higher-order personality factors: extraversion, agreeableness, conscientiousness, neuroticism, and openness to experience/intellect. These factors are closely related to the Myers-Briggs Type Indicator (MBTI) preferences for extraversion, intuition, feeling, and judging, which correspond to extraversion, openness to experience, agreeableness, and conscientiousness, respectively.[13] The MBTI is the most widely used psychological assessment in the world not associated with identifying psychosis.

The first dimension of the MBTI is associated with how individuals derive their energy. A person preferring extraversion tends to be energized by others, and appears sociable, active, and relational. In contrast, an individual preferring introversion is more inwardly energized, preferring time for concentration, typically with fewer relationships and more focused in a concentrated set of interests. Extraversion also relates to higher levels of dopamine, which may be associated with greater risk-taking behavior. Dopamine is associated with the reward system the brain assigns to pleasure. Activities such as enjoying food, sensual pleasures, working out, or playing video games can increase dopamine levels. This association is tied to the relation between dopamine and testosterone, assertiveness, and dominance and is associated with a desire for risk-taking in order to achieve rewards. In an extravert, dopamine may be released as a result of interacting with others regarding investment activity. How does this affect investors' behavior? Interaction with others may result in extrovert investors taking on additional risk.

Another dimension of the MBTI is based on how people make decisions—thinking versus feeling. The MBTI preference for feeling is related to the Five-Factor Model characteristic of agreeableness. Those with the feeling preference value harmony and inclusiveness in decision-making, often considering circumstances in drawing conclusions. In contrast, a person preferring the thinking preference seeks fairness and enforcement of rules and laws above circumstances and tends to be more focused on achievement. Similar to a feeling preference, an individual high in agreeableness tends to be trusting, altruistic, good-natured, empathic, and helpful. Someone low in agreeableness may appear cynical, rude, suspicious, uncooperative, irritable, and even manipulative, vengeful, and ruthless. Empathy shows an association to imitating others' actions. Accordingly, investor strategy can be affected. People who exhibit agreeableness may be susceptible to momentum-based strategies that involve mimicking the actions of the crowd.[14]

Another dimension of the MBTI focuses on how people order their outside world. The MBTI preference for judging is associated with a desire for closure in decision-making. Those with the judging preference are list-driven individuals who are energized by finalizing a decision. The counterdimension to judging is the perceiving preference in which people prefer openness, tend to rush to meet deadlines at the last minute, and are always seeking more information to make better-informed decisions. Conscientiousness, related to judging, refers to the degree of organization, control, persistence, and motivation for goal-directed behavior. Someone low in conscientiousness tends to have less direction and motivation. Conscientiousness is tied to serotonin, which is involved in control and restraint.[15] Because serotonin is considered a natural mood stabilizer, high levels of serotonin are associated with a more strategic focus in decision-making. Thus, a person who exhibits characteristics associated with conscientiousness is less likely to make impulsive investment decisions.

Openness to experience refers to actively seeking and appreciating new experiences. People high in openness are imaginative, curious, and open to unconventional ideas and values. The MBTI focuses on how individuals process information—sensing versus intuition. Openness relates to the MBTI preference of intuition. Intuition is an information-processing manner in which people tend to be oriented to the "big picture," focusing on the overview and then the details. The counterdimension is sensing, in which information processing occurs through the five senses, with a focus on details. Those low in openness share some of these same characteristics, tending to be conventional and dogmatic in beliefs and attitudes, set in their ways, and emotionally unresponsive. Such individuals may be drawn to existing investment strategies that conform to the status quo bias. Openness is positively correlated with performance in working memory and cognitive control tests.[16]

How Do Demographic and Socioeconomic Factors Influence Investors?

Who tends to take the most risk when investing—males or females? If you answered men, you are correct, but why? Women tend to be less financially literate than men. Although some of the difference is attributable to income, the results persist after economic and demographic controls. Income could explain some of the allocation differences found across gender. Men tend to earn higher incomes, and higher-income investors are more willing to take on more risk.[17] Discrimination comes from differences in labor market access, the types of invest ment advice received (women tend to receive more conservative recommendations based on the assumption that they are naturally more risk-averse), and the overall information access in terms of smaller professional networks in which such information sharing takes places. As a result, one gender-based finding is that men take on too much risk and women invest too conservatively.[18] Such generalizations, however, are inappropriate given additional demographic and socioeconomic factors for which gender may serve as a proxy. Differences in wealth, income, employment, discrimination, human capital choices, and preferences all relate to these underlying factors.

Are gender differences tied to marital status? Although marriage alone does not explain differences in risk aversion, significant differences exist when considering the interaction of marriage and gender. In general, single women and married men are less likely to invest exclusively in stocks than single men, who tend to be less risk-averse.[19]

Income uncertainty, which is the proportion of income that is transitory rather than permanent, may best explain the difference in accumulated wealth between groups. For example, a direct relation exists between income uncertainty and risk aversion for African American investors relative to white investors.[20] African Americans are also less likely to have a checking or savings account or hold stock. Moreover, African Americans are less likely to take on less financial risk than other demographic groups.[21]

How does age affect investor decision-making? As a person gets older, the number of remaining working years diminishes and the future income stream lessens. People typically have very limited investable wealth outside of their retirement accounts. For most investors with relatively modest savings, this relation means that their ability to recover from a major market correction is reduced, potentially delaying their ability to retire. Investors correspondingly reduce the risk level of their investments. Potentially offsetting this change is that income levels tend to rise over a worker's life. Higher levels of income generally lead to higher levels of investment risk.[22] Thus, retirement savings to date, income level, and years until retirement are all factors that influence risk-taking ability over time.

How Do Behavioral Biases Affect Sophisticated or Knowledgeable Investors?

Individual investors often look to experts to gain a better understanding of the investment decisions they should make. Experts, such as institutional investors, corporate executives, and financial analysts are often classified as sophisticated or knowledgeable investors. Institutional investors consist of those working for endowments, foundations, pension plans, life insurance companies, property or casualty (nonlife) insurance companies, and banks. Institutional investors are becoming increasingly educated about behavioral finance and inefficiencies that behavioral biases can create in stock markets. However, such knowledge and education does not guarantee that they are free from behavioral biases. The nature of common biases may differ between professional and individual investors. For instance, overconfidence for institutional investors is often tied to their educational pedigree, experience, or certificates and credentials. For these professionals, holding their own behavioral biases at bay allows them to exploit opportunities caused by behavioral biases in the financial markets.

Institutional investors need to understand that despite their mastery of rational market principles, markets may not operate in a totally rational manner. For example, a professional investor may correctly identify a stock that is priced lower than its intrinsic value. However, that does not mean that the stock price will rise to its intrinsic value. In fact, a stock's price can become more mispriced before it moves to its intrinsic value.

Investors' tendencies for behavioral biases have both micro and macro implications. Micro behavioral biases affect individual investors' portfolios. However, institutional investors need to recognize that macro-based behavior may influence the market. Understanding individual behavior helps wealth managers understand the varying range of individual clients and how to best serve each of their needs.

Corporate executives also have behavioral biases. Chief executive officers (CEOs) can exhibit characteristics that render them optimistic, overconfident, risk-averse, and self-interested. In turn, these CEOs may overestimate future earnings growth and underestimate earnings risk, perceiving a larger cost to issuing equity than debt. Such behavior can result in wealth-destroying investments, particularly involving mergers and acquisitions. For example, acquiring a company in an unrelated industry may help expand an executive's empire, but it may not help the company grow. The CEO of a pharmaceutical company likely knows little about how to run a company that produces steel products. Such acquisitions often fail because the CEO lacks the knowledge to strategically compete in an unrelated industry. Additionally, CEOs who are highly risk-averse may fail to choose an appropriate level of debt financing or underinvest, which results in holding high cash balances. If a CEO appears too risk-averse, the board of directors should provide incentives to control the CEO's behavioral biases and increase risk-taking, as well as align CEO and shareholder interests.

Behavioral biases of financial analysts typically concern the reports and recommendations they offer. Analysts' reports may lack independence and objectivity due to conflicts of interest arising from other divisions within their firms, including those of the brokerage house and the banking side. In other words, analysts may feel pressured to issue a buy recommendation if the company for which they work is also in charge of selling new issues of that company's stock. Such a bias hurts small or unsophisticated investors. Investors should consider both the source of analysts' bias and analysts' characteristics that may help investors to select reports based on an assessment of their overall objectivity.

What Types of Behavioral Biases Influence Professional Investors?

Can individual investors, who suffer from behavioral biases, turn to professional investors to mitigate such problems? Not always. Professional investors may suffer from behavioral biases similar to those that plague individual investors, although these biases manifest themselves differently. Overconfidence, the disposition effect, and familiarity bias are common behavioral biases of some professional investors.

Isolating the effects of overconfidence is challenging because it is likely a proxy for other explanatory variables. Overconfidence exists among both individual and institutional investors, but the latter group is less vulnerable. Nonetheless, institutional investors exhibit overconfidence buying more aggressively after experiencing gains.[23] However, gender differences in overconfident tendencies don't seem to exist among professional managers. Experience and investor sophistication could eliminate or at least lessen common behavioral biases based on gender.

The *disposition effect*, which is an investor's tendency to sell winning securities too soon and retain losing securities too long, also exists among professional investors. As is the case with overconfidence, this effect is less pronounced among institutional than individual investors. Evidence suggests that investors' sophistication and experiences eliminate the reluctance to sell losing stocks and also reduce the likelihood of professional investors realizing gains too soon.[24] Thus, more sophisticated institutional investors who possess longer trading experience are less likely to suffer from the disposition effect.[25] Where the effect exists among professionals, it tends to occur among less successful managers and those with less trading experience. Thus, the evidence still aligns with findings that more sophisticated investors are less subject to behavioral biases. Specifically, successful mutual fund managers are more likely to sell their losers than are underperforming managers.[26]

Another behavioral bias exhibited by professional investors is *familiarity bias*, which is the tendency of investors to select investments of companies known to them. Familiarity bias can lead to underdiversified portfolios through, for example, home-biased portfolios in which investors overweight the familiar home market. Home bias and familiarity bias are linked. When professional investors seek out foreign investments, they are still drawn to the familiar.

To What Extent Does Mood Affect Investing and Other Financial Decision-Making Behavior?

Have you noticed differences in how you approach decisions based on your current frame of mind? When you are in a good mood, your outlook is more positive and decision-making tends to be more focused on what is possible. A person in a bad mood often focuses on what can go wrong. Mood and emotion can also influence investors' behavior.

What factors influence mood? Evidence shows that sunny conditions affect mood and that mood affects stock returns. In other words, a positive relation exists between sunny days within a country and returns generated by the market index for that country. Sunny days seem to improve mood, making investors more open to taking risk. Sunshine is certainly a factor that contributes to improved mood. Thus, weather conditions such as sunshine and cloud cover affect investors' behavior.[27] People are more optimistic investors when the weather is sunny and more pessimistic when it is rainy.

Obviously, mood is not exclusively related to weather conditions. A general feeling of goodwill and positive thoughts about the direction of a city, state, country, or world can also influence market performance. For instance, many cite the 1990s as a time of general optimism about the direction of the United States, which was also associated with a period of tremendous stock market performance. Likewise, bad moods can negatively affect stock returns. This state of mind can result in a short-term reduction in the demand for risky assets, which in turn affects stock prices.

How Do Social Interactions and Peer Effects Influence Investing Behavior?

The proliferation of social media has changed how people operate and think. From Facebook to Twitter, the impact of social media on shaping opinions is apparent. From presidential elections to brand marketing, decision-making processes are influenced by what is shared. Social networks, including family, friends, coworkers, neighbors, and others, can influence investors' behavior. Both investment clubs and individuals are more likely to invest in stocks that are associated with a good rationale, such as a company that is on a most-admired companies list. An *investment club* is a group of individuals who meet periodically to pool their money and invest. Having good reasons for recommended stocks tends to be more important to investment clubs because the person proposing the stock affects the wealth of all members. Compared to individuals, groups favor stocks selected on the basis of good reasons, despite the fact that such reasons don't improve performance.[28]

Beyond investment clubs, the behavior of peers, such as friends, neighbors, and coworkers, partly drives the decision to participate in the stock market. The rate of transmission of finance news and rumors through social contacts or networks influences investors' behavior. The forces driving investor networks' effects, such as simple imitation, herding, or biased information transfer, remain unclear. The investment performance of friends and family can also influence the decision to enter the stock market. In particular, good portfolio returns by social networks induce people who previously did not invest in the market to do so.[29]

How Does Herding Affect Markets?

Herding in asset markets occurs when investors mimic what others are doing. This behavior can extend to similar positions within individual securities, within a given industry, and within an entire market. Financial history is filled with examples of herding. During the 1990s, investors drove technology stocks to unreasonably high levels, despite realizing that such stocks were overpriced, because they could not risk being left behind. In early 2000, technology stocks plummeted as the market finally recognized that the herd had driven prices too high. In the mid-2000s, a similar situation developed with real estate, leading to the financial crisis of 2007–2008.

Herding can be associated with irrational behavior of jumping on the bandwagon of a current fad or being motivated by irrational fear. As Dan Rather, an American journalist and the former news anchor for the *CBS Evening News*, once observed, "Once the herd starts moving in one direction, it's very hard to turn it, even slightly." Professional investors are often reluctant to take positions that may be out of line with their peers, fearing that if they are wrong, clients will remember their errant prediction, which makes them look less perceptive than their peers. Going with the crowd offers protection in the sense that clients may be more forgiving if many experts shared the recommendation in question, thus making it a collective error, not an individual one. In other words, professional investors have reputational concerns. If the reasons for herding lack rational justification, then herding could result in moving asset prices away from their intrinsic values, resulting in mispricing and eventually a bubble. However, if herding is based on rational behavior, markets could become more efficient as a result.

Herding behavior exists among professional investors for both asset classes and entire markets. For example, economic forecasters often engage in herding behavior. As Edgar Fiedler, an American economist, once noted, "The herd instinct among forecasters makes sheep look like independent thinkers." In the United States, the herding effect is also observed with individual stocks. Professional investors' trades are related to the trading activity in which they previously engaged and with that of other professional investors' past trades. Such evidence is consistent with the premise that professional investors engage in momentum-based trading strategies. Recall, momentum trading strategies are built on purchasing securities that have recently trended upward and selling securities that have recently trended downward. However, momentum trading only partially explains herding. Herding behavior among professional investors tends to be associated with an information-based rationale, which can create better market efficiency over time.[30]

Herding also appears to affect the market in that a positive relation exists between changes in professional ownership and stock returns. The implication is that herding occurs among professional investors, resulting in a momentum effect that does not appear to reverse itself in the year following the change. Apparently, professional investors create more efficient markets more quickly because they are better informed than individual investors.[31]

Should People Invest in the Stock of the Company for Which They Work?

Investors often believe that the stock of the company for which they work, called *own-company stock*, is an attractive investment. However, it is often a risky strategy for individual investors. If a company experiences financial difficulty, the likelihood of a price decline increases. Likewise, employees are more likely to be laid off. Thus, investing in own-company stock results in additional risk as the performance of the stock and the likelihood of continued employment are highly related. The rationale for this investor decision is that employees "know" their company well and their company is a less risky option than other investments or the overall stock market.[32]

This view, however, is wrong. Not only is own-company investing riskier, such a strategy can result in a disaster for a person's retirement assets. The issue becomes more pronounced over time with the trend away from defined benefit plans, in which investment risk-bearing resides with the employer, to defined contribution plans, in which risk-bearing resides with the employee. A *defined benefit plan* provides retirees with a retirement benefit based on a formula that includes the number of years of service as a percentage of maximum salary or salary over a given time window. A *defined contribution plan* is one in which the employee makes decisions as to how retirement assets are invested and must live with the consequences of such decisions. Employees in stand-alone companies overweight own-company stocks more than employees in conglomerate firms. Loyalty seems to be the primary rationale for the difference. According to one study, this loyalty bias has huge implications for employees, reducing their retirement income by about 20%.[33]

Indeed, loyalty can extend beyond employees to customers. A positive relation exists among a customer relationship, company ownership, and the size of the ownership stake. Customers are more likely to buy and less likely to sell stock of companies of which they are a patron. The longer the association, the stronger is the stock relation.[34]

What Biases Lead Investors to Buy or Sell Certain Mutual Funds?

Mutual funds attract investors for various reasons. From a behavioral standpoint, investors are often drawn to mutual funds with superior past performance. However, past performance does not guarantee that future performance will replicate the past, as pointed out several times. As Christopher Traulsen, a director of fund research at Morningstar Investment Management Europe, notes, "A lot of the companies these funds have invested in have run pretty hard. Chasing performance here is probably a recipe for disaster."

Individual characteristics tend to be associated with mutual fund selection. Those investors more prone to behavioral biases typically experience inferior performance based on their ability to make wise choices about mutual fund style, expenses, turnover, and market timing decisions within the fund. Chasing funds with high past performance is a sign of investors exhibiting their behavioral biases rather than a careful selection process based on identifying funds that exhibit true managerial skill. Additionally, funds with higher fee structures often result in underperformance.

Mutual fund investors tend to exhibit the disposition effect in their realization of gains and losses. They also find evidence of narrow framing for mutual fund investors. *Narrow framing* refers to the tendency to focus on individual investments without considering the overall portfolio. Additionally, mutual fund investors exhibit overconfidence and familiarity bias. They tend to trade too often and unsuccessfully, which suggests overconfidence. Familiarity is measured by *local bias*, which is the distance between the investor's home and the location of the fund's headquarters.[35] Chasing past winners with higher fees and trading more frequently may help to explain the demand for underperforming active mutual funds. Individual investors suffering from behavioral biases are drawn to this subset of mutual fund options.

So which biases explain mutual fund selections based exclusively on past performance? The *hot-hand fallacy* is a belief that mutual fund managers have periods in which they are "hot." In other words, a window exists in which their performance deviates from long-term average performance in a positive way. The concept is not isolated to investing, but also applies to athletic performance. Basketball players and their fans often believe that players have hot streaks in which they outperform their long-term average performance. However, the hot-hand fallacy is indeed a fallacy. Little support exists for the presence of performance persistence among managers of mutual funds.[36]

Investors are not exclusively focused on maximizing returns when selecting mutual fund managers. One potential explanation, analogous to selecting doctors within the medical profession, is that investors place a premium on trust. Consequently, they are willing to pay higher fees to work with managers whom they consider more trustworthy.

Trust becomes increasingly more desirable as the investment option being considered becomes riskier. According to one study, fund managers had a strong incentive to allocate assets toward high-technology stocks during the late 1990s despite the assumption of overvaluation to satisfy the herding mentality existing among investors. After all, the fund manager wanted investors to buy that fund. Such moves, while ultimately not in the best interests of investors, may have helped satisfy their emotional and psychological needs.[37]

5

NUDGE

THE INFLUENCE OF FRAME
DEPENDENCE

How a situation or question is proposed can influence what people think of it. People react differently to "If you quit smoking, you will live longer" than to "If you don't quit smoking, you will die sooner." Although both statements provide the same information, the reaction to the first statement is more favorable. Why? It is more positively phrased because people generally would prefer to live longer. The style in which a phrase is structured is called its *frame*. Using an appropriate frame can help persuade a person to act or to hold a specific opinion. Political pollsters use frames to nudge people toward a particular point of view, as do marketing specialists to affect buying behavior. *Decision frames*, which are the manner in which a question is proposed, are also prevalent in finance, but many are unintentional. Framing can have a dramatic impact on investment behavior and future wealth. This chapter identifies the primary frames in finance and their influence on decision-making.

What Is Frame Dependence?

A discussion of frame dependence can start with prospect theory. According to prospect theory, people behave differently depending on whether they view their investment as a gain or a loss. They are more likely to sell a stock if it has gained in price and less likely if it has declined in price. Assume that you bought a stock for $100 per share two years ago. At the end of the first year, the stock increased to $120. Now, at the end of the second year, the stock price is $110 per share. Do you consider this a gain or a loss?

The answer depends on your reference point. A *reference point*, also known as an *anchor*, for stocks is a price that a person uses to compare with the current price. If your reference point is the original purchase price of $100, then the stock gained $10 per share. If you mentally adjusted the price at the end of the first year to $120, then the stock appears to have a $10 per share loss. The $110 is framed in comparison to a reference point, which in this example is either $100 or $120. So how this situation is framed affects the likelihood of holding or selling the stock. Thus, the term *frame dependence* means that the actions depend on the frame in which the situation is viewed.

Frame dependence influences decisions in many aspects of daily life. For example, experiments show that when you go to the store to buy a camera and only two cameras are available, most people buy the one with the lower price. However, if a third, the highest priced, camera is added to the mix, then people generally pick the middle-priced camera. The store can increase sales of the middle-priced camera simply by having a higher-priced camera available. Thus, a store can increase its sales revenue by having high-priced options available for its products even if no one buys the most expensive ones. When the decision frame includes two choices, the most important attribute is usually price. However, when the frame includes more options, other influences have an effect. In this case, that other influence is often *extremeness aversion*. The lowest and highest priced options seem too extreme, so people buy the middle one. The fact that choices often come in threes, such as Tall, Grande, and Venti lattes at Starbucks, is not an accident.

The tendency to avoid the extreme alternatives is called *extreme* or *extremeness aversion bias*. People often go to considerable lengths to avoid an option that seems extreme. Instead, they tend to choose the "safe option" and take a middle path rather than pick something at the edges. The medium-priced camera or latte just seems safer. The idea of extremeness aversion comes from the research conducted by Daniel Kahneman, a psychologist noted for his work on the psychology of judgment and decision-making, as mentioned in previous chapters. Although taking the safe course of action is often a good strategy in life and investing, the biggest rewards frequently involve an element of risk. Thus, extremeness aversion does not always lead to the best choice.

Let's consider an example involving investments. Assume that you inherited $200,000 and have three choices to invest the funds: (1) put the money under a mattress, (2) deposit it in a bank savings account, or (3) invest the money in stocks. The first or safest option of putting the money under a mattress offers no monetary gain, so you are unlikely to choose it. Instead, you are likely to choose the mid-range option of depositing the money in a bank rather than the riskier option of stocks. Over the long term, a diversified portfolio of stocks is likely to outperform the returns generated from savings accounts. The key lesson from this example is that you need to distinguish between safe and risky options because sometimes the risk is worth the reward. Learning to overcome extremeness aversion means learning when to seek rewards through taking calculated risks.

Frame dependence influences personal decisions, as well as decisions within the investment industry. People can use biases and frame dependence to influence others in ways that could improve their health and wealth over their lifetimes. This idea is referred to as a *nudge* because it provides a free choice but nudges people toward the preferred choice. This chapter illustrates how frame dependence affects decisions and how nudge programs are being implemented in society.

What Is an Example of Frame Dependence?

Frame dependence can occur in the most basic mental processes. Consider the estimation of a multiplication problem.

Nobel laureate Daniel Kahneman and Amos Tversky told participants in an experiment to estimate the answer to a problem in just 10 seconds.[1] Because the problem is too complex for most to solve quickly, it requires making an estimate. The researchers asked some participants to solve the following problem:

$2 \times 3 \times 4 \times 5 \times 6 \times 7 \times 8.$

They gave other participants this problem:

$8 \times 7 \times 6 \times 5 \times 4 \times 3 \times 2.$

The two problems are clearly the same except for the order of the numbers. The simple change of frame by rearranging the numbers had a tremendous impact on the estimates. When the first number was a 2, the average estimate was 512. When the first number was an 8, the average estimate was 2,250, more than four times larger! Thus, the framing of this exercise greatly influenced the responses. Also, note that the starting number in the second problem is four times larger than in the first. People tend to anchor on the first number and estimate using a left to right progression through the numbers. Unfortunately, people are not very good at estimating multiplication problems. The correct answer is 40,320.

How Can Frame Dependence Affect Health Policy?

How questions are framed can strongly affect the decisions people make. Consider the decisions made at organizations such as the Centers for Disease Control and Prevention (CDC) in the United States and the World Health Organization (WHO) when combating the spread of diseases. Here Kahneman proposed the following experiment:[2]

Imagine that the United States is preparing for the outbreak of an unusual disease, which is expected to kill 600 people. Two alternative programs to combat the disease have been proposed. Assume the exact scientific estimates of the programs' consequences are as follows:

A. If Program A is adopted, 200 people will be saved.
B. If Program B is adopted, there is a 1/3 probability that 600 people will be saved and a 2/3 probability that no one will be saved.

Which program would you choose—A or B?

The participants must choose which program to implement. Program A is a certain event and Program B entails risk. However, the expected value of each option is the same. That is, if Program B is picked every time when a similar disease occurs, 200 people will be saved on average, even though some of the time 600 people will be saved and the other times no one will be saved. This average of 200 people saved is the same as the 200 people that will be saved for certain in Program A. Program B is risky because a high chance exists that no one will be saved. In the experiment, 72% of the participants picked the certain results in Program A and only 28% picked the risky Program B.

Where things get really interesting is how people respond to slightly different framing:

C. If Program C is adopted, 400 people will die.
D. If Program D is adopted, there is a 1/3 probability that nobody will die and a 2/3 probability that 600 people will die.

Which of these two programs—C or D—would you support?

These two choices also include a certain option (Program C) and a risky option (Program D). Similar to the first example, these two options have the same expected number of deaths, 400 people. But this time, only 22% picked the certain Program C and 78% chose the risky Program D.

What may not be obvious is that Program A is the same as Program C and that Programs B and D are the same but presented in two different frames. The first set of choices is framed in a positive way—saving lives. The second set of choices is framed in a negative manner—people dying. Framed in a positive manner, about three-fourths of the participants selected the certain option to save 200 people—with 400 dying. When faced with the negative frame, people dying, choosing the option where 400 will die seems too harsh. As a result, nearly three-fourths of the participants chose the risky option, which is the opposite of the positively framed question results. The most common program selected was the opposite choice because of the differences in positive versus negative framing of the options. Thus, decision framing can have a real-world impact on government policy decisions.

How Does Framing Affect Investment Risk and Return Assessments?

A basic finance principle is that risk and expected return are positively related. That is, if investors want to earn higher returns, they must take higher investment risk. If this principle were false, then people could earn high returns from low-risk investments, such as their bank savings accounts, without the need to invest elsewhere. A bank savings account offers a safer, but lower, return. To earn higher returns, people need to invest in riskier assets such as bonds, stocks, and mutual funds. The return or reward for taking risk is called the *risk premium*. Think of the return from stocks coming in two parts, a risk-free return and a risk premium. A *risk-free rate* represents the interest an investor would expect from an absolutely risk-free investment over a specified period of time. In practice, the risk-free rate does not exist because even the safest investments carry some amount of risk, such as inflation. As a proxy, U.S.-based investors often use the interest rate on a three-month U.S. Treasury bill as the risk-free rate. To try to earn a higher investment return, an investor must take higher risk to obtain a larger risk premium. Thus, comparing one stock investment with another is about assessing how much risk the stocks have and matching that risk with the investor's risk tolerance.

Those educated in finance understand this trade-off between risk and expected return. However, people often don't think in terms of this trade-off frame but in terms of what is "better."[3] The better frame measures investments in terms of good and bad, not high risk and low risk. This view is dangerous because an investment that offers high returns and low risk seems better. But that is not how markets typically work. Finding investments with high returns and low risk is highly unlikely. High returns are earned from risk premiums, which entail taking risk.

Thinking in terms of "better" makes people susceptible to scammers who promise super high returns in safe investments. The results of these broken promises are apparent in the form of Ponzi schemes and other types of investment fraud. A *Ponzi scheme* is a fraudulent investment operation in which the operator generates "returns" for earlier investors through funds invested by later investors, rather than from legitimate business activities. Eventually, no new investors are available to supply additional cash to the scheme and it collapses. Bernie Madoff, who is now serving a prison sentence, perpetrated the largest Ponzi scheme in U.S. history, nearly $65 billion! His arrest in late 2008 and the following media frenzy in 2009 captured the attention of the national news for months. Although most Ponzi schemes promise high returns with low risk, Madoff offered very stable returns regardless of market conditions. However, he fabricated all of the returns and used money from recent investors to provide returns to early ones. Investors can sometimes avoid scammers by reframing investment offers in the risk-and-return perspective. When offered a low-risk investment claiming a high return, they should place the investment in the risk premium frame to help them avoid making a mistake or even experiencing a disaster.

Yet most people naturally think of investments as being good or bad, better or worse, but not a question of risk versus expected return, as they should. Even experienced investors can make the mistake of framing the investment attributes poorly. For example, Meir Statman, a finance professor at Santa Clara University, had a group of high net-worth clients of a U.S. investment firm review a list of 210 firms from the annual *Fortune* survey of executives and analysts.[4] One set of investors assessed the riskiness of each firm on a scale of 1 to 10, with 10 being the riskiest. The other group of investors predicted the relative future return of each firm, also on a scale of 1 to 10. Each group ranked either risk or return, but not both. Note that because risk and expected return are related, saying a firm is risky is the same as saying it should earn a high return, and vice versa. Investment professionals know this relation. Merging the two rankings shows firms that the investors ranked with the highest predicted returns also had the lowest risk rankings, on average. Low-return firms had high risk rankings. The two sets of rankings are clearly not linked through financial concepts because the rankings have a relation contrary to that proposed by financial theory. Instead, these investors likely were thinking about which firms were better. Investors ranking on risk thought the better firms must be safer. Investors ranking on return thought the better firms would provide a high return. When the two independent groups of rankings were merged, the better firms had high return expectations and low risk. Although these characteristics rarely ever exist in financial markets, people can make decisions based on this misconception.

Even professionals can fall into this trap. In workshops over a 15-year period, Hersh Shefrin, also a finance professor at Santa Clara University, asked financial professionals for their assessment of popular technology stocks. How did they frame their evaluation? They could use any information they normally access in their valuation processes. Given this comprehensive information and their analysis, Shefrin asked them about the firms' risk and expected return.[5] He found a close association between their risk assessment and common quantitative risk measures.

Surprisingly, these financial professionals reported estimates of expected return that were not positively related to the risk assessment they provided. In fact, in 14 of the 15 years in which Shefrin conducted the experiment, the correlation between the forecast return and risk assessment was negative, which runs counter to financial theory. Even with all their normal investment information available, these financial professionals abandoned the frame of risk versus expected return when forecasting returns. Instead, they used a good/bad or better/worse frame. This natural bias toward framing finance decisions kept these professionals from making good investment predictions.

The framing of a decision can influence the stocks or mutual funds that investors select. A better or worse frame is problematic because it suggests some investments may offer what may seem like better characteristics—high return and low risk. But these characteristics don't exist together in well-functioning capital markets because high expected return is associated with high risk, not low risk. Consider that many people view companies from this better or worse frame. A person may like a company because of its products or its reputation for being a good place to work. The *representativeness heuristic* suggests that an investor will move from liking a company's products or services to believing that it is a good investment. Perception of a better company becomes perception of a better investment.

How Do Decision Frames Affect Investment Predictions?

Consider the difference between framing a change in absolute versus relative amounts, and then extrapolating into the future—that is, making a prediction. The Standard & Poor's 500 Index (S&P 500) is the most popular measure of the stock market's performance in the investment industry. It contains

500 of the largest domestic companies listed on U.S. stock exchanges. Let's ask a forecasting question from two different decision frames. If the S&P 500 rose 20% last year to 2,500, what level is it likely to achieve at the end of this year; what is the likely percentage of return this year? Does thinking in terms of level versus percent return matter?

Some analysts predict a year-end target level, while others forecast a return for the year. Both level and return predictions are asking for the same forecast information, but from different frames—levels versus returns. The two different frames elicit nontrivial differences in responses. When predicting a level, people provide a lower estimate, on average, than is implied by the estimated return. For a return of 10%, the S&P 500 Index that started at 2,500 would increase by 250, to 2,750. Decision-framing by asking for the return causes analysts to predict a return of 10%. But if asked for a prediction on level, they are likely to provide a lower estimate, such as 2,700. Why? This result occurs because two different biases influence the two frames. When predicting using price levels, people tend to use a mean reversion, or even a reversal trend.[6] *Mean reversion* means that levels tend to revert over time to an average. So, when an index moves an extreme amount up or down, people tend to predict a reversal to "even out" on average. However, when using returns or changes to make forecasts, they are more likely to extrapolate the current trend. This difference is a form of the representativeness heuristic.

Surveys often ask people to make economic predictions. Some surveys, such as the Michigan Survey of Consumers, ask for future returns. Others ask for predicted price levels, such as the Livingston Survey of the Federal Reserve Bank of Philadelphia. Analysts frequently make forecasts about future earnings, dividends, and stock prices, but also forecast growth rates. Note that forecasting earnings, dividends, and stock prices is likely to evoke mean reversion, while people forecasting growth rates are more likely to use extrapolation. Thus, an analyst may experience extrapolation or mean-reversion bias depending on whether prices or returns frame the forecast.

How Does Framing Affect Retirement Accounts?

The most common pension plan offered in the United States is a *defined contribution plan*, which is called a 401(k) plan for corporations. To set up the plan, employees must decide whether to participate. If they do participate, they must also decide how much to contribute in pretax dollars and how to allocate the money to various investments. The employer may also contribute to the employee's plan. Retirement benefits depend on how much the employee and employer contributed, the length of time of the investment, and the investment rate earned. People rarely change their pension plan preferences once they set them up. Therefore, the framing of decisions at the initiation of the pension plan may have a detrimental financial impact on employees if it causes them to make poor choices.

Historically, employers have made many mistakes in how they frame the pension plan for new employees. A human resources department would often issue a large information packet with much technical jargon on the choices available and ask new employees to review the material, complete the forms, and return them to start the plan. This approach led many new employees, often more than half, to not start a pension plan.

This process describes an opt-in design. There are major differences in how people respond to opt-in and opt-out frames. A good example is the organ donor program in countries around the world. In a typical organ donor program in the United States, drivers are asked if they want to be an organ donor when they get a driver's license. This is an opt-in frame because drivers must decide to participate. Alternatively, Sweden considers its citizens to be organ donors unless they opt out of the program. The difference in rates of participation is dramatic. In opt-in countries such as the United States,

Germany, and the United Kingdom, participation rates are less than one-quarter of the population. In opt-out countries such as Sweden, Austria, and France, participation rates are around 90%.[7]

Reframing the defined contribution plan decision from an opt-in to an opt-out process leads to an equally dramatic impact. One 401(k) plan that changed its process to an opt-out design saw new employee participation rates jump from 37% to 86%.[8] Although an automatic enrollment policy results in substantially more employees participating in the pension plan, they tend to choose the default level of contributions and default asset allocation. As previously noted, people rarely change their plan after setting it up. Therefore, if the default contribution level is very low, say 2%, or the default asset allocation takes little risk and therefore offers little return, then employees may not be saving enough to fund their retirement. Those who would not have contributed at all are better off with the automatic enrollment. However, employees who would have opted into a pension plan might have selected a higher contribution rate and a more aggressive asset allocation. The opt-out plan actually harms those who simply use the default levels. Therefore, designing the optimal opt-out plan entails a moderate contribution rate and an appropriate mix of investments suited to the employee's age.

Besides the opt-in versus opt-out frame, another decision frame problem occurs with the number of investments available from which to choose. Too many options can overwhelm a new employee. Only a small portion of the population, especially among younger people, has investment knowledge. Thus, hundreds of investment choices may delay the initial plan decisions so long that employees never enroll. According to research estimates, every 10 mutual funds added to a 401(k) menu decreases the probability of an employee participating in the plan by 1.5 to 2.0 percentage points. Thus, fewer choices are better.[9]

Another problem is investment risk. Pension plan systems have trouble framing the investment risks, and people don't fully understand how much risk they are willing to take. When people don't know, they tend to be "extremeness averse." In other words, when in doubt, pick an option that appears moderate. This reaction is the response mentioned in the camera example at the beginning of this chapter. It also applies to people choosing how to allocate their pension contributions.

A demonstration shows this effect.[10] First, assume you are given some statistics on the risk and return of three investment choices, labeled A, B, and C. The risk clearly increases with each option, so C is the highest-risk investment. How are you likely to rank these alternatives? Evidence suggests that fewer than 30% will favor the most risky investment, option C. Now let's change the choices by deleting the safest option, A, and adding an even more risky option, D. What option would you now choose—B, C, or D? Evidence shows that more than half will select Option C, which now looks like a less extreme choice with more moderate risk. In other words, people often don't really know what level of risk they want to take. Therefore, they make the moderate choice. So when the question is framed with safer choices, people want to take less risk. When they are faced with riskier choices, they want to take more risk.

Can Frame Dependence Affect Social Security Choices?

The decision of when to start receiving Social Security (SS) benefits has important wealth implications for retiring U.S. citizens. The benefits paid depend on the contributions taxpayers make throughout their lives and the age they begin receiving the payments. Starting payments at the earliest age possible of 62 achieves the lowest cash payments. If the person waits until an older age, the payments are higher. The payment increases each year until age 70. When someone has enough financial resources to choose when to start her SS payments, should she start earlier or later? The longer someone waits, the higher the person's monthly income will be. That phrase is stated in a positive, or gain, decision frame.

Before 2008, the Social Security Administration illustrated this decision through a break-even analysis. The break-even analysis pits receiving lower SS payments earlier against delaying for years and receiving higher payments later. How long would someone need to live while receiving the higher payments in order to make up for the missed payments forgone when delaying initiating SS? This decision frame focuses the retiree on the loss of delaying being balanced by timing of death. Both missing payments and the timing of death are negative frames. Instead, the decision could be framed in a positive way: the longer a person waits to start receiving SS benefits, the more monthly income she receives.

Can this subtle gain versus loss framing affect a person's decision on when to start receiving SS benefits? Evidence shows that such decisions are sensitive to how the information is presented.[11] The results indicate that framing the choice using gains rather than losses causes a later claim age. When the example anchors on an earlier age, such as 62, participants make a claim at an earlier age. Additionally, people who are less financially literate and have lower earnings are more susceptible to being influenced by these decision frames. According to these findings, the presentation of information can have an important influence on the decision when to start benefits. That decision affects the level of monthly income for as long as the recipient lives. Hence, sometimes a seemingly small decision can change your life forever.

How Can Banks Use Frames to Increase Saving?

Economists and governments are very interested in helping lower-income households change destructive behavior and develop financially sound habits. Low-income families in the United States have very low savings, yet they frequently play the lottery. They believe that lotteries are a more likely path to wealth than saving. Thus, some savings and loan associations and credit unions have enacted lottery-linked savings accounts to boost saving behavior.[12] Depending on the program, each savings account deposit or bond purchased enters the customer into a weekly or monthly lottery. That is, people buy into the lottery drawing through saving behavior. Lottery prizes are one large cash award and several small cash awards. To fund the program, the savings institution offers a slightly lower account interest rate and uses the cost savings to fund the cash awards. Those who are loss-averse value the structure of these programs because they attach the excitement frame from gambling to savings behavior. Yet lottery entries have small costs (the lower interest rate) that are less transparent than the larger and more visible losses of spending cash for lottery tickets.

In Michigan, Commonwealth (formerly the D2D Fund) implemented a program called "Save to Win" through several credit unions.[13] Every $25 that savers deposited gave them an entry (up to 10) into monthly cash prize drawings. Over time, the entries also accumulate for additional entries to win an annual $100,000 grand prize. The program created $8.5 million in savings the first year. The program has been expanded to 12 states, and $140 million in savings has accumulated through 60,000 accounts. Commonwealth has used this experience to design other types of savings structures linked to prizes. In 2016, Commonwealth teamed up with Walmart's MoneyCard and MoneyCard Vault. Each dollar transferred from the MoneyCard account to the Vault equated to one entry into the national drawing. This program had the advantage of being in a place that people from low-earning households frequent, Walmart.

Some of these programs are very large and have existed for decades. For example, the Premium Bond program in the United Kingdom began in 1956.[14] More than one million prizes are given at each lottery drawing. Most of the prizes are small, consisting of more than a million prizes of £50 each. But the program also has two prizes worth £1 million each. To participate, a saver must make a minimum £100 deposit. The

Premium Bond program has amassed more than £30 billion in savings. More than a quarter of British households participate. Other international programs include those in Central America and South America. These programs give away cars and have daily drawings. If you have trouble building a savings account, look for these lottery-linked savings programs in your area. Credit unions, savings and loans, and even Walmart are places to look.

Can These Savings Programs Use Peer Pressure to Increase Savings?

The social environment frame can be a powerful influence on financial decisions. One aspect of social influence comes from peer pressure. Many people use peer pressure to help make better decisions. They may choose to have a workout partner or a study buddy. Knowing that a workout partner will be waiting at the gym is a strong motivator to get to the gym. Others use formal weight-loss groups, and the peer pressure that comes with them, as a device to reach their goals. Why not use peer pressure to help commit to higher savings rates? Two international studies show how this can work.

In many countries, low-income citizens are entrepreneurs by necessity. In a program to boost savings in Chile, researchers randomly assigned low-income entrepreneurs to three groups.[15] The first group, the peer group, is the one of interest. These people could publicly announce their savings goals to the others in the group. The second group was offered a savings account that provided a 5% annual real rate of return. The last group was the control group, whose members were offered the basic savings account that provided a 0.3% annual real rate of return. Both the peer group and control group received the basic savings account. Weekly savings progress was measured against the participants' stated goals and recognized their progress in weekly meetings. The control group had a low savings and participation rate. The second group, consisting of the people offered the high interest rate account, also had a low participation rate. A higher interest rate did not seem to motivate them to start saving. However, those in the peer group increased their savings behavior 3.7 times more than the Control Group. Apparently, the social frame had a greater impact on saving behavior than did the gains (higher interest rates) frame.

This social environment had two important influences. The first was the aspirational impact of seeing the social group members experience success. The second influence was peer pressure. Which influence drove the savings behavior? Researchers conducted a second experiment to try to separate the two influences. They implemented this experiment using electronic messaging systems, rather than weekly face-to-face meetings. The messages informed the group of the progress of everyone's saving goals. Not everyone received the same message. To disentangle the two effects, one group was assigned a savings buddy and provided information about that buddy's progress. The second group did not have an assigned partner, but its members received information updates on the group's progress. The results show that the groups had comparable savings behavior. Both the aspirational effects and peer pressure had similar influences on savings patterns. Thus, the social environment frame can influence savings decisions in different ways.

Another international program took place in Israel. Historically, Israel's national pension system required employees to contribute to their own pension plan, and the money went into an investment fund that the employer selected. A national pension reform in 2005 allowed employees to make their contribution to any of more than 200 investment fund choices.[16] Who changed investment funds and why? From a behavioral perspective, the opportunity to change investment funds was not well framed. As discussed earlier in the pension plan sections, going from one mandated fund to a choice of hundreds of funds overwhelms many people. Because the employees are not required to make any changes, status quo bias also affects the decision. *Status quo bias* is a preference for having things remain the same, making no changes. In the end, only 7% of the employees changed investment funds.

Why did the 7% change investment funds? Interestingly, no investment characteristics of the funds they switched from or to stand out in the analysis. The funds to which the employees changed had not earned higher returns, charged lower fees, or had different services. This program is similar to one that took place in Chile in which the group of entrepreneurs who could opt for a savings account with a higher interest rate did not save any more than the control group with a low interest rate. As with the experiment in Chile, the social frame also appears to be a motivator.

This program shows that peer pressure influenced the Israelis who changed investment funds. A strong association exists between an employee's new fund selected and the funds selected by coworkers with whom they are likely to socialize. Specifically, this association occurs among employees within a department and is stronger for employees of the same ethnic group. A survey of the employees that changed funds reveals that they knew little about their new fund's investment characteristics other than coworkers recommended it. Thus, the social aspects of the decision frame had a greater influence on the selection than information about the fund. People who are faced with a decision should examine the investment information carefully to offset the large influence that social pressures may have on that decision.

How Is Frame Dependence Used for Charitable Giving?

Philanthropy is a big industry. Many large organizations seek to help society in one way or another and depend on contributions from people who share their values. Organizations such as the American Cancer Society and the United Way create national and local events to enhance charitable donations.

Noncharitable organizations, such as hospitals and universities, also have active development programs. What motivates people to make a donation? Donors are likely to receive a warm feeling of satisfaction by helping others in a manner that is meaningful to them. But what is the source of that satisfaction? Knowing the source can lead to optimal framing of the donation "ask."

People receive many solicitations asking for donations for worthy causes. The text and images try to illustrate the great need for a donation and elicit emotions that motivate. However, many of these solicitations are missing what may be the strongest driver of charitable giving—social recognition. People are particularly concerned with the visibility of their positive behavior. Fundraisers can increase donations by giving donors public attention, especially when that recognition sends a signal about their altruism. However, the prospective donors must know about the social attention in advance. That is, the frame of asking for the gift must include the form of public acknowledgment. When it does, charitable organizations receive more donations. This difference occurs at the smallest contribution levels. That is why so many people are willing to donate a dollar to the local animal shelter to see their name printed on a paper bone stuck to the wall.

At higher levels of donation, the giving circle is a good example of the effect of recognition. Many organizations that seek donations recognize their donors in tiered levels such as bronze (lowest), gold (moderate), and platinum (highest), determined by the size of the gift.[17] Thus, the organizations can frame their sales pitches to potential donors in these levels. Notice the availability of three tiers, which is common, and remember the impact of including a high-priced camera or riskier investment option. Although few may donate at the platinum level, its existence may influence people to increase their donations from the lowest (bronze) to the moderate (gold) level in this frame. Donors seek the prestige of being publicly recognized at their level, especially when they give more than the basic level.

Public recognition has two aspects: providing social image benefits and offering an opportunity to lead others. The first aspect allows the donor to say, "See how generous I am." The second aspect says, "Donate too and follow my lead." This second aspect may be related to peer pressure, except that the organization is having the donors provide the social pressure for prospective donors. Between the social image benefit and the social leadership benefit, social image is the primary driver of the giving circles.[18]

One way to understand framing is to assess the quality of the decision frames being presented to you on a daily basis. For example, you are likely receiving frequent solicitations for donations via TV ads, mail ads, crowdfunding emails, and so on. Which provide the strongest salient images or stories? Which solicitations frame giving in tiers? Which ones provide for public recognition? Being able to spot and understand the behavioral influences directed to you will allow you reduce their impact on your decisions.

How Does the Framing of Return Information Affect Decisions?

Consider a mutual fund that has been around for a long time producing many months of high, moderate, and low (negative) returns. What is the best way to present this information? The presentation of the return distributions can affect the investment choices made. One important aspect for society is how people direct their pension assets. People who take little risk find that their portfolios are unlikely to grow substantially even decades later. However, risky investments are volatile, which means that periods of negative returns will occur, which concerns those who are loss-averse. As a result, people often fail to allocate pension assets to the stock market. Framing return distributions one way may push investors to take less risk, such as by entirely avoiding the stock market. Yet framing returns in other ways may help them choose a more diversified portfolio.

According to prospect theory, people are both loss-averse and view gains and losses individually through a narrow framing process. This means that losses emotionally impact most people more than gains. A good investment portfolio diversifies by including investments that have low positive or negative correlations with each other. That is, the investments tend either to move independently from each other or to move in opposite directions, thus reducing a portfolio's volatility and risk. The individual investments may have high volatility, but the portfolio of combined assets has much lower volatility, which is the purpose of diversification. Thus, displaying investment return data in individual assets or funds instead of an aggregate portfolio may lead to people taking less risk.

For example, the survey firm Qualtrics presented nearly 250 people with different frames of individual and aggregated return distributions.[19] The participants could change the allocations to four funds: (1) an international stock fund, (2) a domestic stock fund, (3) a domestic bond fund, and (4) a money market fund. The participants could then see the return distribution for their selection. Some people saw the return distribution of the individual funds, while others saw the distribution of the portfolio they had created. The participants then changed the asset allocation to the funds until they had the portfolio characteristics they wanted. The group that saw the segregated returns selected a portfolio whose equity proportion was 4.2 percentage points lower, on average, than the group seeing the portfolio level return distribution. Because this experiment was computer driven, it identified those people who spent a substantial amount of time studying the return distribution. From this subsample of participants taking more time, the equity proportion decline was nearly 10 percentage points lower for those seeing the segregated returns. Therefore, examining individual assets characteristics instead of aggregate portfolio characteristics may lead you to taking less risk, and thus earning a lower return.

Return information can be displayed through other dimensions. For example, would showing a fund's annual return each year for the last 10 years or as two annual five-year averages matter? In other words, does displaying long-horizon portfolio returns at infrequent intervals rather than short-horizon returns in every period affect investors' choices? Shorter interval returns are more volatile. That is, larger losses and larger gains are shown in individual month returns than in average monthly returns over long periods. Because losses affect investor psyche more than gains, shorter interval returns lead to more risk aversion and lower-risk portfolios.[20] This finding is important because lower-risk portfolios over long periods lead to lower returns and less wealth.

A good illustration of how investors react to the display of returns occurred in 2010 when the Israeli regulatory agency governing the retirement-savings market, which is similar to U.S. 401(k) plans, changed how it displayed information.[21] Before the change, the agency prominently showed one-month returns on monthly statements. The regulator then prohibited the display of retirement funds' returns for any period shorter than 12 months. After the policy change, investors saw the 12-month return every month, including the 12-month return from both this month's statement and last month's statement. From this information, an investor could compute the one-month return. However, although the one-month return information is still available, it is much less salient than previously. A change in behavior can be examined by comparing how investors reacted to the fund returns before and after the regulatory change. The shock to the information display caused the following change in behavior: fund flow became less sensitive to short-term returns, overall trade volume decreased, and investors allocated more to riskier funds.

These results are consistent with people exhibiting *myopic loss aversion*, which occurs when someone is both loss-averse and has a tendency to evaluate outcomes frequently. The simple change in framing return distributions led to a change in portfolio risk allocation that could have a big impact on the retirees' total accumulated wealth. As a result, you should try to minimize viewing investment performance in its most volatile frames, which are individual assets, short-term performance, and returns. So, to avoid myopic loss aversion, try to review your investments as a portfolio instead of individual assets. Also try to examine long-term returns, say, over three or five years, instead of monthly or annually. In addition, view the portfolio level, in dollars, instead of returns. These habits will help you avoid the short-term myopic behavior that leads to poor decisions.

What Is the Nudge Revolution?

If the framing of information and choices can trick people, should the government or a company choose for them? Many cultures, particularly the United States, have been built on the premise that people have the freedom of choice. The attitude is that individuals know what is best for them. The libertarian ideology advocates maximum individual liberty. However, others hold different views. On the other side of the spectrum is paternalism, in which an authority makes decisions for others "for their own good." In fact, people often don't know what is in their own best interests. They frequently don't even know their own preferences. Additionally, psychological biases, cognitive errors, and framing influence their decisions and can cause them to make bad choices. Yet having the government mandate what citizens do is distasteful to many. This background sets the stage for the concept of "nudge" and the 2017 Nobel Memorial Prize in Economic Sciences.

In their book *Nudge: Improving Decisions about Health, Wealth, and Happiness*, Richard Thaler and Cass Sunstein describe how freedom of choice and government help can be combined.[22] They call this ideology *libertarian paternalism* and contend that people should have the right to choose, but that the decision should be framed in such a way as to "nudge" them in the best direction. Thus, the *nudge revolution* is the deliberate use of choice architecture to frame decisions so that people act to improve their own welfare. The use of nudge choice architecture can influence health, social, environmental, and financial decisions and habits. For example, some have designed interventions to increase the number of people getting a flu shot, exercising more, stopping smoking, and increasing savings. An attractive nudge policy is one that increases engagement in a desired behavior by a larger amount per dollar spent than a traditional intervention. The desire for an attractive nudge policy is why Sunstein recommends having a Council of Psychological Advisers to the government, similar to the traditional Council of Economic Advisers.[23] The United Kingdom established a nudge unit in 2010 and the United States established the White House Social and Behavioral Sciences Team in 2015. Thaler won the Nobel Prize in 2017 for behavioral economics and the nudge concept.

How Are Framing Concepts Being Used to Lure People into Bad Financial Decisions?

Advertising and marketing have been trying to nudge people in one direction or another for decades. However, problems occur when people are manipulated to make poor financial choices. Those who visit any payday lender can see psychological nudges everywhere. Payday lenders offer very small, unsecured short-term loans called *payday loans* at high interest rates. The industry gets its name because borrowers may receive a few hundred dollars to be repaid in a couple of weeks when they receive their next paycheck. In-store advertisements mention that it costs $15 for a $100 loan. However, the loans are for two weeks and typically average $350 in size. Thus, the narrow frame tries to hide the fact that, given the way the loans work, this loan represents an annual rate of more than

6,000%. Payday loans require borrowers to pay the financing fee in advance. So, in this example, the borrower receives $85 and must repay $100 in two weeks, which is a 17.65% cost in just two weeks. If the borrower is unable to pay back the loan and rolls over the loan every two weeks to the end of the year, the amount due is $5,815. On average, borrowers need more than nine consecutive loans to pay off the debt.

Would a different frame help potential borrowers make a different decision or pay back the loan sooner? A survey of borrowers reveals that it can.[24] The survey provides borrowers with different information sets, including the true dollar cost of a loan over different time periods, or the annual percentage rate of their loan compared to other types of loans, or the time needed to pay back the loan. The analysis finds that all three frames reduce the chance that the borrower takes out another similar type loan. However, the strongest results occur with framing the cost in dollar terms. The impact is an 11% reduction in the likelihood of repeating the loan. If the government wants to nudge these borrowers away from the extraordinarily high costs of payday loans, then policies requiring specific lending frames should help.

How Did Lenders Use Framing to Nudge Homebuyers into Dangerous Mortgages that Led to the Financial Crisis of 2007–2008?

The nudge idea has encouraged cleverly designed programs that use people's own behavioral biases and cognitive errors to benefit them in their finances and health through choice architecture. But, of course, unscrupulous individuals can also create programs to exploit these biases in ways that financially harm people. Actions taken by predatory subprime mortgage lenders provide a good example. A *subprime lender* specializes in lending to borrowers who have a tainted or limited credit history. Before the financial crisis, they designed products that adhered to the law but tricked borrowers by hiding important characteristics of the mortgage contract. Borrowers tend to focus on a few salient dimensions of mortgages, such as the initial closing cost and initial monthly payments. Lenders designed contracts with artificially low closing costs and initial monthly payments that seemed attractive but hid the real costs in other aspects of the mortgage.

Subprime lenders exploited three major psychological biases: (1) people have difficulty processing complex contracts, (2) they underestimate future costs, and (3) they are optimistic about their future ability to pay loans. The first psychological problem is the difficulty of processing complex contracts. The paperwork required for any mortgage is immense. Information overload becomes a problem with hundreds of pages of legal contracts and use of jargon. Thus, people generally focus on just a few prominent features to make a decision. The number of salient items upon which they concentrate decreases during emotional stress, including anger, annoyance, embarrassment, fear, and frustration. In addition, cognitive aging affects the decisions of the elderly, especially for complex decisions.[25] *Cognitive aging* refers to the gradual deterioration of mental skills, including awareness, information handling, memory, and reasoning needed to carry out any task from the most simple to the most complex. Unfortunately, lenders frequently targeted the elderly for exploitation.

The second psychological problem—underestimating future costs—occurs because people have trouble projecting the future through mathematical functions containing exponential terms, such as how interest rates compound over time. This phenomenon is called *exponential growth bias*. Instead, people linearize these functions, which causes them to underestimate future costs.[26] In other words, when a process expands exponentially, people tend to think of it as only expanding as a straight line. They underestimate not only the future value of savings, and thus are not motivated to invest, but also the costs of borrowing.

The third psychological bias is optimism about the future. People generally believe that they will earn more money next year, get a promotion or a better job, and have a better ability to pay loans. Subprime lenders get borrowers to commit to spending that extra money on bigger loan payments, even though that additional income may never arrive. Lastly, subprime lenders played on borrowers' optimism one more time by suggesting that if they couldn't afford the future mortgage payment, they could refinance the loan. Unfortunately for these borrowers, as the mortgage crisis progressed, the market for subprime mortgages collapsed and homeowners could not refinance.

To exploit these biases, subprime mortgage originators designed complex contracts with deferred costs.[27] In this situation, a *deferred cost* is one that a borrower has already incurred but will not repay until later. The complexity of the contract caused the borrower to narrowly frame the decision to a few salient items that originators could easily manipulate. The main characteristics of the contract included closing costs, interest rate, monthly mortgage payment, and total cost over the life of the loan.

Consider the traditional 30-year, fixed-rate mortgage. To understand this mortgage, a prospective borrower can focus on the monthly payment and closing costs. In contrast, the new subprime mortgages were more complex because they initially had low teaser rates that rose one or two years later. A *teaser rate* is a low, adjustable introductory interest rate advertised for a loan designed to attract potential customers. Teaser rates are often too good to be true for the long term and are far below the realistic rate for the loan. Borrowers could also finance the closing costs by adding them to the loan principal. *Closing costs* are expenses in addition to the price of the property in a real estate transaction. Common closing costs include loan origination fees, points, prepaid homeowners' insurance, appraisal fees, inspection fees, transfer taxes, escrow fees, attorney fees, deed-recording fees, credit report charges, prepaid interest, prepaid private mortgage insurance, title searches, and title search costs. Using a teaser rate and financing the closing costs lowered the initial monthly payment and made the costs appear very small. The initial monthly payment was temporary and increased substantially, even doubled, when the interest rate reset. The optimism of many borrowers led them to believe that they could afford those payments in two years, or at least be able to refinance the mortgage at that time.

Some subprime mortgages drove down the monthly payment even further using negative amortization. *Negative amortization* is an increase in a loan's principal balance caused by making payments that are not large enough to cover the interest due. Negative amortization causes the loan balance to get larger after every payment instead of smaller. Thus, the remaining amount of interest owed is added to the loan's principal, which ultimately causes the borrower to owe more money. For example, at the end of the 30-year mortgage, the borrower may still owe a large payment called a *balloon payment*. This feature added more complexity to the mortgage.

In addition, loan costs were much higher than normal because, when they are added to the loan balance, the borrower pays interest on them over the loan's life. Adding the costs to the principal hid the magnitude of those costs. Because adding these closing costs to the principal obscured them, the lenders added many more fees. As many as 15 official-sounding fees added thousands of dollars in costs. With smaller second mortgages, these fees added up to as much as 20% of the loan amount. Recall from prospect theory that people have diminishing disutility, or dissatisfaction, to losses. In other words, they feel worse paying two costs of $100 each than paying one cost of $200. Treating each fee separately would create more disutility but by bundling the small fees, the lender soothes the borrower's dissatisfaction. So the borrower is more likely to agree to pay all the fees when they are bundled than when listed separately.

Besides having trouble with compounding, people have difficulty understanding how small differences in percentages in the compounding lead to large differences in costs.

When people assess percentages, they often think of the possible range of 0% to 100%. On that large scale, an increment of less than a percentage point seems inconsequential. So the difference between 10% and 10.8%, for example, seems minor. But a change from 10% to 10.8% increases the monthly payment on a 30-year mortgage by nearly 7%. This scale problem also occurs when adding the closing costs to the principal. For example, the difference between a closing cost of $2,500 and $6,000 seems large. Adding it to the loan principal of $250,000 increases the loan balance of $252,500 to $256,000 and does not seem so large. So adding thousands of dollars in closing costs greatly benefits the loan originator, but hiding that cost in the principal tends to go unnoticed by borrowers.

Charging fees that are added to the principal also increases one of the salient aspects of the mortgage—initial monthly payments. Therefore, the industry evolved new techniques to drive down the initial payment, including negative amortization. Framing the mortgage contract to encourage borrowers to focus on initial payment and closing costs that brokers manipulated, brokers could earn high origination fees. An *origination fee* is an upfront fee charged by a lender for processing a new loan application. Of course, these terrible contracts took their toll on borrowers. In fact, many borrowers could not afford the monthly payments after the teaser rate expired. When housing prices started to decline, lenders could no longer refinance these homes. In 2001, early in the housing bubble, the delinquency rate for these subprime mortgages was 10%, but by 2008, the default rate had climbed to nearly 40%.[28]

As stated above, three major psychological biases that might be exploited are (1) people have difficulty processing complex contracts, (2) they underestimate future costs, and (3) they are optimistic about their future. So, when considering financial products, be wary when they seem overly complicated. That might be intentional and designed to frustrate you until you get to the point that you just want to complete the process. Also, costs are often framed as many seemingly small and

insignificant expenses. Instead of looking at each item separately, you should focus on the total, which is a better picture
of a product's true costs. Lastly, beware of arguments that you
will be able to pay more in the future because of potential increases in your income. Committing to pay more in the future
based on hope usually turns out badly.

How Can Employers Use Nudging Concepts to Help Improve Pension Plan Decisions?

Biases can be exploited by decision architecture to help people
make better choices beyond the initial nudge of a decision.
Again, consider the typical process for a new employee to sign
up for a defined contribution pension plan, such as a 401(k)
plan. The employee visits the human resources department
and opts in to the plan by determining how much to contribute
and where to allocate the contribution among the investment
options. An employee wanting to make a change must initiate
the change through human resources, which can be a cumber-
some process.

Several psychological biases inhibit employees from opti-
mizing their 401(k) plans. For example, framing the contribution to the plan as a paycheck deduction would not appeal to
someone who is loss-averse. People don't like to see their pay-
checks decline. In addition, status quo bias causes employees
to procrastinate. They may not go to human resources either
to initiate the pension plan or to change it later. However, this
process can be improved to help employees get signed up and
increase their contribution over time.

Richard Thaler and Shlomo Benartzi designed just such a
plan, which they called Save More Tomorrow (SMT).[29] The
program's name denotes the use of behavioral finance by providing the positive frame of "save" instead of the negative
connotation of "contribute." Because the name also expresses
the bias that people are more willing to commit to an action
they will do later than one they must do now, it uses the term

"tomorrow." The program is designed for employees who are not currently contributing to their pension plan.

The SMT plan consists of four steps. The first step of the program is to ask the employee to agree to the plan months in advance. For example, the employee agrees now, but the first contribution does not occur for several months. Actually, the first contribution happens at the employee's next pay raise. The second step is to begin the pension contributions with a small amount, say 2%. Having the employee split the raise with himself may be ideal. For example, if the next pay raise is 6%, then both the pension contributions and the employee's paycheck would increase by 3%. This approach avoids the feeling of loss aversion because the paycheck does not decline when the contributions begin. The third aspect of the program is to have the employee agree to increase the pension plan contribution at every pay raise until reaching the maximum level. Again, these increases would occur well into the future and not cause a decline in the paycheck. Lastly, the employee can opt out of the program at any time. People need that level of comfort to initially agree to the SMT program. The expectation is that status quo bias will inhibit them from doing the paperwork to opt out.

The researchers selected a midsized company with a low saving participation rate to test the SMT program. The 315 employees of the manufacturing company had an average 401(k) plan contribution rate of 4.4%. To provide a control sample for the experiment, the company asked all employees to increase their contribution rate by 5 percentage points over their current rate. The company offered the SMT program to the 207 employees who claimed they could not afford the reduction in their paycheck to accommodate the increased contribution rate. Of these 207 employees, 162 joined the SMT program. The 153 employees not joining the program had an average contribution rate of 5.3%. These employees either made no changes or made a one-time increase in their contribution rate. At the end of the study, they had increased their contribution rate from 5.3% to

7.5%. The employees who did adopt the SMT plan started with a low average contribution rate of 3.5%. However, after three pay raises, their contribution rate increased to 11.6%. The SMT program benefited these employees because they dramatically increased their contribution rate and thereby increased their financial resources for retirement. Well-designed programs such as SMT use decision frames and behavioral biases to help people make decisions that improve their lives.

Can Nudging Be Effective?

Nudging behavior is commonplace at both an individual and a policy level. An advantage of using a nudge is that it is not coercive, so those affected don't view the nudge as infringing on their freedom. Take the example of Danica Patrick, who dropped out of high school to pursue a career as a race car driver. She became the first woman to hold the lead during the Indianapolis 500. When asked about her career, she said: "I'm not feeling like I was pushed into this. . . . I feel like I should be doing this. I feel like this is where my life should be headed. And sometimes we just get kind of nudged there. Sometimes it's big nudges, and sometimes it's little."[30]

At the policy level, governments frequently try to motivate citizens to change their behavior. They can coerce people to act in their own best interest, such as by enacting seat belt laws and issuing fines. Too much coercion can infringe on individual freedoms and endanger politicians' position in a democracy. Alternatively, economic incentives, such as tax incentives, subsidies, and other financial inducements, are traditional policy tools. For example, governments sometimes make tuition deductible and provide tax credits to help eligible children attend college. Regarding energy conservation, the government can provide discounts to households that use less energy than the prior year. However, economic incentives can be costly. For example, those who purchased all-electric and plug-in hybrid cars in or after 2010 could be eligible for a federal income tax credit of up to $7,500. The federal solar tax credit, also known as the investment tax credit (ITC), permits deducting 30% of the cost of installing a solar energy system from one's federal taxes. The ITC applies to both residential and commercial systems, and no cap exists on its value. A third option is to use behavioral strategies to nudge people into desired actions.

A nudge choice architecture should be inexpensive and easy to implement. If a nudge policy increases the engagement in a desired behavior at a lower cost than traditional economic incentive strategies, then it is an attractive use of resources. Therefore, a cost-benefit analysis of nudge strategies is appropriate. *Cost-benefit analysis* is a systematic process for calculating and comparing benefits and costs of a decision, policy, or project. Thus, the benefit of getting more people to engage in the desired behavior can be compared to the program's cost. The government wants more people to contribute, and contribute more, to their defined contribution plans. It has used the tax code to provide the economic incentives through the tax deferred status of the contributions.

For example, one program, working with the Department of Defense, sent an email to 806,861 military service members who were not contributing to their pension plan, some of whom received the nudge message and some of whom, those in the control group, did not.[11] Although the campaign cost just $5,000 to implement, 5,265 of the people nudged started contributing to their pension plan. The increase in savings amounted to $1.3 million in the first month and an estimated $8 million for the year. Therefore, the cost-benefit ratio of this inexpensive nudge is impressive, as the program prompted more than one person for every $1 spent on the program. In addition, every $1 spent on the program prompted $1,600 in new investment.

What is the cost-benefit of the government's promotion through making pension plan contributions tax deferred? If an employee in a 25% marginal tax bracket contributes $1,000 for the year, a $250 tax savings occurs. This $250 is a cost to the government because it is a loss of tax revenue. Thus, the government tax deferral policy generates only $4 in savings per $1 spent. Many programs have tried to increase savings rates. A nudge program required new employees to indicate their preferred pension plan contribution rate during their first month. It conservatively generated $100 of additional savings per $1 spent. The cost of an opt-out program is essentially zero. Other economic incentive-based saving programs offer either $20 to attend an information fair[32] or a matched contribution for a savings deposit.[33] These programs only generated $14.58 and $5.59 per dollar spent, respectively. Clearly, the nudge programs are more economically efficient than the economic incentive programs.

A team of scholars reports cost-benefit analysis for traditional and nudge programs in different areas.[34] For example, various traditional interventions target increasing college enrollment. The federal Social Security Benefit Program ended its subsidy, and college attendance among the affected students dropped by 18.2%.[35] The average cost per eligible person was $5,181, and $28,571 per college enrollee. Similar programs at the state level using voucher programs cost $196,078 per college enrollee.[36]

Now compare the success rate of these programs to a nudge program in which H&R Block tax professionals filled out the Free Applications for Federal Student Aid (FAFSA) forms for its clients' high school seniors. This program only cost the tax preparer's time, about $53 on average. Yet it produced additional college students at a cost of only $654 per enrollee.[37] The nudge program at H&R Block was much more economically efficient at getting high school seniors to attend college.

Nudge programs seem to be more efficient in other areas too. In energy conservation, a nudge program sent letters to households comparing their energy use to that of their neighbors. This program used the frames of social norms and competitiveness. Over two years, this intervention saved 27.3 kWh per dollar spent.[38] Conversely, using economic incentives,

California utilities asked residential customers to reduce energy consumption. Any household that reduced energy consumption by at least 20% compared to the last summer received a 20% rebate off its bill. The program saved only 3.41 kWh per dollar spent.[39]

In summary, nudge programs can be useful tools to increase socially desired behaviors. They neither coerce nor limit freedom of choice, and they can be very cost effective.

6

COGNITIVE ABILITY

Billionaire investor Warren Buffett is known for his pithy insights. He once observed that in finance "you don't need to be a rocket scientist. Investing is not a game where the guy with the 160 IQ beats the guy with 130 IQ." He also said that "if you have more than 120 or 130 IQ points, you can afford to give the rest away. You don't need extraordinary intelligence to succeed as an investor." Although being smart has advantages, the difference between a person with very superior intelligence (IQ between 120 and 140) and a genius or near genius (IQ above 140) may be unimportant. Nonetheless, considerable evidence shows that cognitive ability is very important to making good decisions. As Buffett also comments, "Rationality is essential when others are making decisions based on short-term greed or fear."[1] Buffett's comment about the importance of being rational is exactly right. Although many words, such as "genius," "street smart," "educated," "rational," and "experienced" imply intelligence, these terms may refer to different kinds of intelligence that are generated from various types of cognitive processing. No matter how smart a person is, cognitive ability is sometimes degraded such as during periods of sleep deprivation or for the elderly. This chapter explores the consequences of making financial decisions with different cognitive abilities, competencies, and factors affecting cognitive functioning.

What Are the Cognitive Processes Involved in Investing?

The process of making investment decisions is complex. It involves evaluating the risk of an investment and how that investment affects a portfolio. The sophistication of many traders, the interconnectedness of global markets, and the complexity of financial instruments all influence investments. Although intelligence seemingly should play an important role in being a successful investor, different types of cognitive processing exist that could relate to investment decisions. The three types of cognitive processing applicable to financial decisions are fluid intelligence, cognitive reflection, and the theory of mind.

- *Fluid intelligence* refers to the more traditional measure of intellectual abilities that can be measured by the intelligence quotient (IQ). This number represents someone's reasoning ability as compared to a norm or average for a person's age, taken as 100. Thus, IQ is a good indicator of a person's computational capacity compared to the average population. Individuals with higher IQs may be better able to handle the mathematics associated with finance and investing.
- *Cognitive reflection* is the inclination to take more time and effort in reasoning. People who use a less effortful mode of reasoning are making more intuitive decisions. This thinking mode often uses heuristics and behavioral biases to facilitate quicker decisions. An analytical thinking mode requires more cognitive effort. An investor who engages in more effortful reasoning is more likely to avoid specific behavioral biases and make more rational decisions.
- The *theory of mind* refers to a person's capacity to infer others' intentions. Because investing and trading involve assessing the true worth of assets using incomplete information, and the amount of information differs among people, being able to infer when other people have more information from their actions can be very valuable.

How Does IQ Relate to Investment Success?

The participation rate in the stock market is surprisingly low. Only about half of U.S. households invest in the stock market through stock ownership, equity mutual funds, or retirement accounts. Even fewer Europeans are stock market investors. Stocks are a common investment asset class for building wealth over time because they typically generate a higher return, albeit with more risk, than investments such as a savings account at a bank or bonds. The jump from being a saver who saves money through a bank or other means to an investor is often characterized by participation in the stock market. Considerable evidence shows that people with higher fluid intelligence are more likely to be both involved in the stock market and more successful.

Let's look at the results of studies involving the link between IQ and investment success. Specifically, there is a positive relation between increases in IQ scores and increases in stock market participation. In fact, IQ appears to account for most of the difference in the stock market participation rate, instead of income, wealth, and other characteristics. Additionally, the high-IQ men chose superior portfolios that are more diversified.[2] IQ also affects stock trading profits and portfolio selection. The portfolios of high-IQ investors substantially outperform those of low-IQ investors. This higher return stems from the higher-IQ investors exhibiting better market timing and stock-picking skills as well as more effective tax-loss selling than low-IQ investors. In other words, higher-IQ investors are better able to buy low and sell high (market timing), buy better-performing stocks (stock picking skills), and sell stocks with losses at the end of the year to lower their taxes (tax loss selling). Lower-IQ investors are more prone to the *disposition effect*, which is the tendency to hold losers too long and sell winners too soon.

One aspect of intelligence is executive function. Executive function skills are the self-management skills that help people manage emotions, organize work, and adapt as circumstances change. This fluid intelligence is an important driver of participating in the stock market. That is, higher intelligence is associated with both directly owning stocks and indirectly owning them through mutual funds.[3]

In general, people with higher fluid intelligence (IQ) are more likely to invest in the stock market. They also appear to be better at investing than those with low fluid intelligence. However, as Warren Buffett notes, "The most important quality for an investor is temperament, not intellect. You need a temperament that neither derives great pleasure from being with the crowd or against the crowd."

What Are the Differences between Analytical and Intuitive Thinking?

Nobel laureate Daniel Kahneman describes two different modes of cognitive reasoning: thinking fast and thinking slow.[4] *Thinking fast* refers to the intuitive thinking mode. Intuitive thinking relies on feelings, heuristics, and relating past experiences to form opinions and make decisions. *Thinking slow* refers to the analytical thinking mode or what he calls reasoning. It occurs when computing multiplication, such as 13 times 157. Kahneman uses the example of a piece of chocolate that has been formed in the shape of a cockroach. Thinking analytically, a fan of chocolate would assess the data at hand and decide to eat the chocolate. Yet an intuitive thinker would be reluctant to eat the chocolate because the cockroach image is linked to unpleasant thoughts or feelings. The intuitive mode of thinking is spontaneous and effortless (fast), while analytical thought is deliberate and takes effort (slow). Due to its effortless aspects, people make most judgments and choices intuitively.

Consider driving to work in a carpool. When the conversation in the car is small talk, the driving requires only effortless cognitive processing. These intuitive activities of driving and simple conversation processing can occur simultaneously because the brain can handle these undemanding cognitive processes at the same time. When either the conversation or driving task requires more cognitive capacity, such as a political debate or parallel parking, the driver must switch to an analytical thinking mode. So the conversation becomes interrupted or the driver becomes distracted. This situation is why texting while driving has led to many accidents. Financial decisions tend to be more complex than driving. Investment decisions often require dealing with uncertainty, diversification, asset allocation, market efficiency, and risk versus expected return, which are analytical tasks. This investment environment requires a high cognitive load, and thus analytical thinking is better than intuitive thinking.

Everyone can think in either mode. However, most people tend to default to one mode or the other. For example, as a generalization, engineers tend toward analytical thinking, while artists and creative types lean toward intuitive thinking. In many cases, those who predominantly make decisions using the analytical mode might make different financial choices than intuitive thinkers. Intuitive thinkers are inclined to use more heuristics to allow for a faster thinking process. However, using heuristics and having behavioral biases are likely to lead to poor financial decisions. Thus, analytical investors use more rational cognitive processes.

How Can Someone's Cognitive Reflection Be Easily Revealed?

Are you quick to go with your gut feeling about an issue and be decisive, or do you like to take time to reflect a little longer before acting? *Cognitive reflection* is the ability not simply to think fast, but also to stop and think slow. Important differences occur among people in their ability to forgo their initial inclinations. In fact, Professor Shane Frederick has designed a simple test with only three math questions, which require analytical thinking to reach the correct answer, to measure whether someone tends toward an intuitive or analytical thinking mode.[5] When Frederick gave the test to various groups, he found that students at the Massachusetts Institute of Technology (MIT), one of the world's leading engineering schools, averaged 2.18 questions correctly out of three. Engineers are apt to be analytical thinkers. By contrast, the average correct answer by a Harvard University choir group was only 1.43, which suggests leaning toward using the intuitive thinking mode. Activities on the internet seem to foster the intuitive mode. Frederick shows that an online sample of people averaged only 1.1.

The three simple questions are called the cognitive reflection test (CRT). The idea of the CRT is to create questions that immediately induce an impulsive answer that happens to be wrong. Getting to the right answer requires a more deliberate thinking process. A quick, impulsive answer indicates that the person tends toward intuitive thinking. A correct answer suggests that the person is using analytical thinking. People with two or three correct answers tend to be analytical thinkers, while those giving two or three incorrect answers tend to be intuitive thinkers. The three questions are the following:

1. If it takes 5 machines 5 minutes to make 5 widgets, how long would it take 100 machines to make 100 widgets? (Note: a *widget* is an unnamed gadget considered for purposes of a hypothetical example.)
2. In a lake, there is a patch of lily pads. Every day, the patch doubles in size. If it takes 48 days for the patch to cover the entire lake, how long would it take for the patch to cover half the lake?
3. A bat and ball together cost $1.10. The bat costs $1.00 more than the ball. How much does the ball cost?

Take this test and get your answers. The first question has a certain rhythm to it. The 5, 5, and 5 rhythm creates an impulsive answer of 100, 100, and 100. So the impulsive answer is 100.

However, the correct and analytical answer is 5 minutes. For the second question, the words "doubles" and "half" lead to a quick answer of 24 days, which is the impulsive answer, but the correct answer is 47 days. If the patch of lily pads doubles each day and covers the lake in 48 days, then the lake must have been half covered the day before (day 47) so that when it doubles, it covers the entire lake. In the third question, the numbers $1.10 and $1.00 are visible and elicit the quick answer of $0.10. However, the $1.00 does not represent the cost of the bat but the difference between the cost of the bat and the cost of the ball. Thus, the ball must cost $0.05, which is the analytical answer. The CRT is scored by the number of correct answers, which all require analytical thinking. So a CRT score of zero or one suggests the person is an intuitive thinker, while a CRT score of two or three classifies the person as an analytical thinker.

The extended CRT adds four questions. These four additional questions can be used on their own when the original three questions become too well known. Or all seven questions can be used for the best reliability. The newer questions are the following:[6]

4. If John can drink one barrel of water in 6 days, and Mary can drink one barrel of water in 12 days, how long would it take them to drink one barrel of water together?
5. Jerry received both the 15th highest and the 15th lowest mark in the class. How many students are in the class?
6. A man buys a pig for $60, sells it for $70, buys it back for $80, and sells it finally for $90. How much has he made?
7. Simon decided to invest $8,000 in the stock market one day early in 2008. Six months after he invested, on July 17, the stocks he had purchased were down 50%. Fortunately for Simon, from July 17 to October 17, the stocks he had purchased went up 75%. At this point, Simon has
   A. broken even in the stock market.
   B. moved ahead of where he began.
   C. lost money.

Now answer questions 4 through 7. Answering question 4, most people will have the initial intuition to average the two numbers and provide an answer of nine days. However, John can drink the barrel in six days alone. With Mary's help, they can perform the task faster. The answer is four days. In question 5, the intuitive answer is 30 students. The more reflective answer is 29 students because the class had 14 students who had better marks and 14 students who had worse marks than Jerry, plus Jerry. For question 6, the intuitive thinking process tries to add the difference for each transaction and arrives at $10. Yet the pig is bought twice for a total of $140 and sold twice for a total price of $160, for a $20 profit. Lastly, question 7 exploits the effect of percentages in gains and losses. The appearance is that losing 50% and then gaining 75% would put Simon ahead of where he began. But if the $8,000 lost half of its value, dropping to $4,000, then Simon would need a 100% return to break even. Thus, Simon lost money.

Both the CRT and the extended CRT measure an individual's tendency toward a first thinking mode. By now, you are likely to have a good notion of whether your thinking style leans more toward the analytical or the intuitive. The next question describes the investment risk and behavioral biases associated with using analytical and intuitive modes. Thus, you will learn what to consider when making your own financial decisions. A strong intuitive thinker may be able to switch to an analytical mode or vice versa. Yet switching modes takes deliberate effort. Also, people may not be as effective or comfortable thinking in their secondary mode.

How Do Analytical and Intuitive Thinking Relate to Behavioral Finance and Investment Performance?

Higher scores on the CRT indicate that a person defaults to an analytical thinking process. Such people tend to perform better on financial metrics. For example, those scoring higher on the CRT earn higher trading profits.[7] Note that trading is different from investing. Investing is usually a long-term activity that considers investment characteristics, such as asset value, risk, and expected return. Alternatively, trading tries to capture short-term price changes and is often related to an asset's supply and demand. Good traders watch the buying and selling of others. If you observe a person continually buying, you might infer that the person is aware of good news about the stock that would be associated with increasing demand for it. People with higher CRT scores tend to be better at inferring other traders' intent and thus earn higher profits.

One reason for the higher profits is that cognitive reflection is important to avoid commonly observed heuristics and behavioral biases such as the base rate fallacy and conservatism bias.[8] The *base rate fallacy* occurs when someone places too little weight on the original or base rate of possibility. *Conservatism bias* is a mental process where people cling to their prior opinions or forecasts, disregarding new information. People with higher cognitive reflection scores are less likely to fall prey to the base rate fallacy and conservatism bias.

To illustrate, first consider the base rate with this question: "In a city with 100 known criminals and 100,000 innocent citizens, a surveillance camera exists with automatic face recognition software. If the camera sees a known criminal, it triggers the alarm with a probability of 99%; if the camera sees an innocent citizen, it triggers the alarm with a probability of 1%. What is the probability of filming a criminal when the alarm is triggered?" The answer is only 9% because it triggers on 99 of the 100 criminals, which is 99% of them, and 1,000 of the innocent citizens, which is 1% of them. So if everyone in the city walked by the camera, they would trigger the alarm 1,099 times, and 99 of them would be criminals, or 9%. For those who are mathematically inclined, the answer is computed as (= [0.99 × 100] / [0.99 × 100 + 0.01 × 100,000]). Common answers to this question are probabilities greater than 90% because they focus on the 99% without fully taking into account that even though the false positive is low, the number of people who could trigger the false positive is far greater than the number of criminals. A *false positive*, also known as a *false alarm*, mistakenly indicates that the condition of interest is present. People with higher CRT scores are more likely to identify that the probability is 10% or less.

How Are Better-Trained and More Experienced Investors Likely to Behave?

Are better-trained and more experienced investors more likely to be risk-averse or risk seekers? *Risk aversion* is a preference for a sure outcome over a gamble with higher or equal expected value. Conversely, the rejection of a sure thing in favor of a gamble of lower or equal expected value is called *risk-seeking* behavior.

According to prospect theory, people tend to choose the certain option when it is framed in a positive manner and choose the risky option when framed in a negative way. Consider the following two questions involving prospect theory:

- Which investment payoff would you pick? Receive (A) $100 for certain or (B) a 50% chance to receive $300 and a 50% chance to receive nothing.
- Which investment payoff would you pick? Lose (A) $100 for certain or (B) a 50% chance to pay $300 and a 50% chance to pay nothing.

The first question is set in the positive domain, as the certain payoff of $100 is less than the expected value of the gamble, $150 (= 0.5[$300] + 0.5[$0]). The difference of $50 might be considered a *risk premium*, which is the reward for taking risk. The second question is set in the loss domain and has the certain alternative with a higher expected value than the gamble.

Are your responses similar to those of experienced investors? For the first question, in the positive domain, research evidence shows that intuitive financial planners tend to select the certain choice (A). But in the loss domain question, they generally select the risky option (B).[9] Although this behavior is consistent with prospect theory, analytical planners tend toward the opposite behavior.

Research findings provide some important implications for decision-makers.[10] First, all people don't have the same level of risk aversion. Instead, they can be risk-seeking in one situation and risk-averse in another. Second, intuitive thinkers are more likely to behave along the axioms of prospect theory than are analytical thinkers. Third, analytical people have a tendency to be more patient than intuitive people. Fourth, people with lower cognitive reflection (intuitive thinkers) are less likely to take financial risk.

What Are the Implications of the Cognitive Process Called Theory of Mind?

Have you ever played the board game Clue or seen or participated in a murder mystery party? In these fun games, the players have some information about who committed the murder. They proceed through the game by asking questions to acquire more information to solve the mystery. Asking a good question is a direct way to get new information. A good player also indirectly acquires information by listening to the questions other players ask and thus infer what they already know. Correctly inferring what others know allows you to solve the mystery first and win the game. In this case, the winner is using the cognitive processing of theory of mind.

The *theory of mind* refers to a person's capacity to infer others' intentions. Uninformed traders can quickly infer the signals of informed traders through their behavior. That is, they can figure out the intent of other traders through their trades, and thus guess the information they must know. This type of intelligence is important in the finance arena.

Let's consider a trading game designed to determine whether people use the theory of mind while participating in financial markets.[11] Consider that you start the game with some cash and can allocate that cash between a bank savings account with a known savings interest rate or two stocks that could pay a dividend between $0 and $0.50 each. You don't know the exact amount each stock will pay, but together, the two dividends add to $0.50. Although you don't know what the dividends will be, you do know others in the game have been given that information. If one game player knows that the dividend of stock B will be above $0.35, then this player also knows that stock A will pay less than $0.15. In this case, owning stock B is better than owning stock A. The trader with inside information will buy more of stock B. If you did not have insider information, you can watch other traders and try to infer what information they know. If you detect a trader buying stock B, you can assume that trader was an insider and knew stock B was worth more than its current price. Observing this, you would also buy stock B. This inference of information is top-of-mind cognitive processing.

By watching people play this game, one can conclude that people are rather good at inferring information from observing the trades of others, despite their lack of formal financial training. Those playing the game who don't have insider information can correctly forecast the price direction about two-thirds of the time, which illustrates that they can correctly identify the informed trader and adjust their trades accordingly.

Of course, not all game players are likely to be successful in following the trades of the insider. What characteristics are associated with successful payers? The success in inferring the information held by other traders comes from top-of-mind processing, not fluid intelligence, which shows that different types of intelligence are not always substitutes for each other. For example, someone who is not good at mathematics can still have strong top-of-mind processing ability and be very successful at some financial activities.

What Is Cognitive Aging?

Have you ever observed what happens to someone's cognitive processes as the person ages, such as a parent, relative, or friend? Sure you have. You probably concluded that some cognitive functions decline over time as a normal aspect of aging. A common misconception, however, is that all cognitive abilities decline with age and that little can be done to alter this decline. In fact, some cognitive abilities, such as vocabulary, are resilient to brain aging and may even improve over time. Other abilities, including conceptual reasoning, memory, and processing speed, gradually decline over time. *Cognitive aging* affects not only the basic processes of learning and memory but also the complex higher-order processes of language and intellectual competence.

The decline in cognitive ability is also associated with a decrease in financial literacy. Although seniors are generally aware of this problem, they don't always recognize the magnitude of the decrease in the ability to manage their own finances.[12] A team of scholars from the Federal Reserve, New York University, and Harvard University estimate that cognitive ability peaks around 20 years old and then declines by 1% per year.[13] However, the rate of financial mistakes takes on a U-shape because it requires both cognitive ability and investment knowledge and experience. In other words, financial decision-making improves with age and peaks in the early fifties despite a person's slowly declining cognitive ability. This situation occurs because of the accumulation of experience, knowledge, and wisdom over time. Still, the incidence of financial mistakes increases after the early fifties due to the ongoing effects of cognitive aging. The incidence of dementia dramatically increases after age 60. Among people older than 80, about 30% have dementia and another 30% experience cognitive impairment without dementia.

Examining the characteristics of loans taken by people of different ages illustrates a U-shape in financial mistakes.

Researchers find that among a group of prime borrowers, middle-aged people borrow at lower interest rates and pay lower fees than both younger and older people. *Prime borrowers* are those who are considered a below-average credit risk because they have a history of using credit wisely and handling loans responsibly. For example, in home equity loans and lines of credit, middle-aged people pay as much as a 0.5% lower annual percentage rate (APR) than younger and older people.

Using credit card balance transfer offers is an interesting case illustrating the difference in fee structures. Nearly everyone has experienced a credit card company offering to transfer the balance from an existing card to a new card. The offer often has a very low interest rate, called a *teaser rate*, often for a six-month period. The teaser rate, however, is only for the transferred debt. New purchases are charged a higher interest rate. Additionally, all monthly payments are used to pay down the transferred balance at the teaser rate, while the new debt accumulates at the higher rate. Thus, the optimal strategy is to make all new purchases on the old credit card during the teaser rate period of the new card, then transfer the balance. About one-third of the people transferring their balance seem to recognize this optimal strategy. Approximately another one-third start making new purchases on the new card but, after one or more pay cycles, discover the higher interest charges and then implement the optimal strategy. The final one-third never discover the optimal strategy and make purchases on the new card throughout the teaser rate period.

How does age factor into using the optimal strategy? Nearly half of young people and older people never discover the optimal strategy, compared to about 30% of middle-aged borrowers. Middle-aged individuals are also more likely than the other two age groups to discover the optimal strategy immediately. If they fail to do so, they are more likely to discover it during the teaser rate period than the other age groups.

The societal impact of cognitive aging is an important issue for much of the developed world because it is experiencing an aging population. In the United States, people in the baby boom generation, born between 1946 and 1964, are reaching retirement age. In fact, they are retiring at the rate of about 10,000 per day. The demographics in Europe are similar to the United States, and the aging in the Japanese population is even further along. How cognitive aging affects the portfolios of a rapidly aging society may have major ramifications for the wealth and income of the retirees. Additionally, this generation represents a large portion of society's wealth. Therefore, their investing preferences and behavior will have serious implications for stock markets.

Does Cognitive Aging Make Seniors More Susceptible to Financial Fraud?

Seniors are particularly at risk for financial *fraud*, which a serious crime that implies deception and a breach of confidence or trust. They have accumulated wealth over decades and have likely reached their peak level of wealth. Thus, the size of potential fraud is greater for seniors than other age groups. Retirees must also manage this investment and the income it provides, which differs from their experience of managing work income and building wealth through making pension contributions. Lastly, cognitive aging affects a senior's ability to make good financial decisions.

The Certified Financial Planner (CFP) Board of Standards reports that older Americans are "subject to unfair, deceptive or abusive financial practices and the problem is pervasive." This board gathers information from thousands of financial advisors with the CFP designation about their clients' experiences.[14] More than half of the advisors have at least one client who has been subject to abusive practices. Half of the advisors have a client who has been offered a "no-risk or low-risk" high-yield investment offer. Financial theory precludes the possibility of an investment expecting a high yield with low risk. So a promise of a low-risk investment that will provide a high return is a warning sign that it is fraudulent. Their clients have also been pitched "You have won a prize!" scams and been subjected to financial abuse by guardians. Common financial exploitation comes in the form of variable annuities, variable life insurance, and whole life insurance. These financial products are combinations of insurance and investments and commonly have very high fees. The size of the scams experienced by elderly clients is substantial. Some extreme losses skewed the average to about $140,000, while the median loss was a still-substantial $50,000. The *median* is the middle value in the list of numbers. Thus, in this example, 50% of the losses were below $50,000 and 50% were above $50,000.

Other scams come in the form of affinity fraud, Ponzi schemes, foreign lotteries, Veterans Affairs benefits fraud, and Social Security or Medicare fraud. *Affinity fraud* is a scheme in which the perpetrator targets a specific group, such as a religious, ethnic, or professional group, and the elderly with the intention of scamming them out of money. Sometimes a few group members unwittingly spread the word about the "opportunity" to other members. This creates a trust that would not ordinarily occur when interacting with a stranger.

How much does cognitive aging play a role in financial fraud?[15] Information collected by the Rush Memory and Aging Project, which is an ongoing longitudinal study that began in 1997 and enrolls more than 1,500 participants from the Chicago metropolitan area, provides some potential answers. Participants are given risk factor assessments and clinical evaluations each year, which include cognitive tests. One important question is whether in the past year they became victims of financial fraud or were told that they were. This process allows for the examination of whether the participants have experienced cognitive declines, based on annual cognitive tests, and how any decline relates to experiencing financial fraud. The unfortunate conclusion is that a decline in cognitive ability of about a third increases the odds of being a financial fraud victim by a similar percentage.

Apparently, cognitive aging also affects behavioral habits and opinions that can increase susceptibility for fraud, as illustrated by the questions used in the Rush project to measure it. Specifically, susceptibility is measured by five questions with answers on a seven-point scale that ranges from strongly disagree to strongly agree, plus a sixth question that is answered yes or no.

1. I answer the phone whenever it rings, even if I do not know who is calling.
2. I have difficulty ending a phone call, even if the caller is a telemarketer, someone I do not know, or someone I did not wish to call me.
3. If something sounds too good to be true, it usually is.
4. Persons over the age of 65 are often targeted by con artists.
5. If a telemarketer calls me, I usually listen to what they have to say.
6. Are you listed on the National Do Not Call Registry?

Combining the answers to these questions into an index and comparing that to the level of cognitive aging leads to the conclusion that declining cognitive ability increases susceptibility to being scammed.

How does cognitive aging affect behavioral biases that might also increase the chance of being scammed? For example, overconfidence plays an important role in falling victim to financial fraud; a 34% increase in overconfidence increases the odds of being scammed by 26%. This relation is even stronger for older victims. The other behavioral bias of interest is the propensity to take risks to break even after a loss. If you tend to take more risk in an attempt to get back to even, that could affect your chances of being scammed. Although risk aversion generally increases with age, fraud victims slightly decrease their risk aversion, making them more susceptible to additional fraud overtures. Indeed, a common "follow-up" scam is to offer fraud victims the opportunity to get their money back for a substantial fee. Those experiencing a decline in cognitive ability tend to increase their risk-taking as a response to being a financial fraud victim.

How Does Getting Older Affect Risk Tolerance?

As the preceding section mentions, risk aversion generally increases with age. Several reasons help to explain why people tend to take less risk as they get older. First, seniors have different investment needs than younger people. Early in life, a person invests for capital growth to save for the future. In retirement, a person has a shorter time horizon and needs income from investments. Another reason for this change in risk behavior is a change in cognitive processing—cognition tends to decline with age. Remember that higher intelligence is associated with less risk aversion. That is, those with higher cognitive ability are willing to take more financial risk and are more likely to invest in stocks. Thus, differences in financial risk aversion between younger and older individuals could stem from different needs, varying cognitive ability, or both.

To separate the role of age-related needs and cognitive ability, one study uses the Survey of Health, Ageing, and Retirement in Europe (SHARE).[16] The survey encompasses more than 12,000 people aged 50 or older and includes questions about age, financial risk attitude, stock market participation, and cognitive skills in math, verbal fluency, and memory. An index of these three cognitive abilities is a strong predictor of whether people invest in the stock market and the level of financial risk they are willing to take. After controlling for age, an individual's willingness to take risk increases with higher levels of cognitive ability. The three measures of cognitive ability have different levels of impact on risk aversion. The math-oriented test had the strongest correlation with willingness to take risks. Verbal fluency was also a strong predictor of risk-taking. The memory test had only a marginal association with risk aversion. The study concludes that cognitive ability drives the association between age and risk attitudes. The financial risk aversion related to getting older is more related to cognitive aging than any change in financial needs.

How Does Cognitive Aging Affect Portfolios?

Because cognitive aging affects a person's decision-making ability and risk aversion, portfolio choice is likely to be affected. However, getting older is also associated with gaining investment experience, which similarly influences portfolio construction. So which effect dominates as investors get older—cognitive decline or investment experience? A peek at people's discount brokerage accounts can show the relation between portfolio holdings and trades in the context of experience and age.[17] Specifically, portfolio characteristics including performance, trading, and diversification can be compared to investors' age and experience.

This examination leads to several fascinating findings. First, older investors are more risk averse, as evidenced by their decisions to hold less risky portfolios. Second, increased experience leads to better investing characteristics, including greater diversification, less frequent trading, increased propensity for year-end tax-loss selling, and fewer behavioral biases. Third, after controlling for experience, older investors exhibit diminished stock selection ability and poorer diversification, consistent with cognitive aging effects. These poor investment decisions lead to poor portfolio performance. Declining cognitive ability results in an estimated 3 percentage points lower risk-adjusted return each year. Older investors, who typically have larger portfolios, underperform by 5 percentage points per year. Over time, investors both gain experience and lose cognitive ability. Experience improves investing skills. At some point, when cognitive aging gets more pervasive, that skill starts to diminish. Investment skill tends to deteriorate sharply starting at the age of 70, on average. These findings imply real economic consequences to cognitive aging.

How Does Cognitive Aging Affect Behavioral Finance?

People use simple rules, called *heuristics*, to make complex decisions. Heuristics simplify the decision and are useful because of the limits on the brain's ability to retain and process information. Do the number and type of heuristics employed by younger and older people differ? Yes, heuristics differ with age.[18]

People make important, complex decisions throughout their life cycle. They must choose investments, and those choices may change because their preferences shift over time. They also must select healthcare options and, at age 65, among different coverages available through Medicare. Simplifying the decision allows you to make it from a reduced amount of information. Of course, you are likely to make a poor decision if you eliminate too much important information.

Elderly people tend to discard some important information about the decision at hand. For example, consider picking a mutual fund company. The number of funds offered by the mutual fund company is of only moderate importance. More important is the cost of the funds, their risk levels, and their performance. If this is too much information to fully assess, then you are likely to use a heuristic, such as picking the mutual fund company with the most funds available or choosing the fund with the best recent performance. Using heuristics is related to the poor decision-making that occurs as people get older. Seniors tend to examine less information, consider fewer options, and count the number of positive attributes provided by each option. Older people are also more easily manipulated through the way others present choices to them.

How Does a Lack of Sleep Affect Cognitive Ability and Financial Decision-Making?

Do you think you get enough sleep? If you are like most people, the answer is no. Going without adequate sleep has both short- and long-term consequences. In the short term, sleep loss can affect your quality of life. It can also affect judgment (cognitive ability), mood, and the ability to learn and retain information, as well as increase the risk of serious accidents and injury. In the long term, chronic sleep deprivation may lead to health problems including obesity, diabetes, and cardiovascular disease. Not surprisingly, insufficient sleep can affect financial decision-making.

Lack of sleep has been linked to major disasters, including the nuclear accident at Chernobyl and the explosion of the space shuttle *Challenger*.[19] On a much smaller scale, the one hour of sleep lost in the switch to daylight saving time in the spring is associated with an increase in traffic accidents, fatal vehicle crashes, pedestrian injuries, and workplace injuries.[20] Sleep loss weakens the part of the brain used for decision-making and leads to less thoughtful actions and heightened social risk-taking. Insufficient sleep reduces responsiveness to incoming stimuli, resulting in reduced attention, and inhibits neural activity. The impairments in psychomotor function resulting from sleep deprivation are similar to those produced by consuming alcohol. That is, physical characteristics of severe sleep deprivation include reduced balance and fine motor skills. Anyone who travels east and loses sleep due to time zone changes can attest that this transition can affect sleep patterns. Sleep patterns can be disrupted for between two days and two weeks, with the average being about one week.[21]

The most consistent effects of sleep deprivation include reduced attention and increased variability in behavioral responses. The impact of insufficient sleep on decision-making is complex because making a decision often does not rely solely upon analytical cognitive processes. Emotional factors that lead to using heuristics often bias judgment processes.[22] Because sleep deprivation alters mood and emotional functioning, the decision-making process is thus changed, altering a person's assessment of risk and decisions.

Sleep problems are a risk factor for developing depression. Because both depression and bad moods can affect financial decision-making,[23] poor sleep quality can influence financial risk-taking. Studies that examine whether global loss of sleep in society can affect the overall stock market reveal mixed results.[24] One study examines the effect of the changing length of daytime through the year in six countries. It finds that as the days get shorter, people suffer from seasonal affective disorder (SAD) and have a heightened risk-aversion that affects stock market returns.[25]

Those studies examine the macro impact of insufficient sleep on the financial markets. To many people, the effect of sleep deprivation at the individual level is most important. A lack of sleep is associated with socially risky activities such as using cigarettes, alcohol, and drugs. Experiments have assessed whether insufficient sleep also translates to increased financial risk-taking.[26] They conclude that sleep deprivation leads to poor financial decision-making and lower financial risk-taking.

What do you do when you must stay awake? If you are like many people, you drink coffee or tea or consume a can of Red Bull. All of these drinks contain caffeine. Does caffeine restore cognitive function? Evidence suggests that financial decision-making remains impaired despite using stimulants after sleep deprivation.[27] Thus, coffee may make you feel more awake, but it doesn't improve your cognitive function when you are sleep deprived.

What Is Cognitive Dissonance and How Does It Manifest Itself in Practice?

Have you ever made an investment decision that resulted in a loss and then rationalized it to relieve mental discomfort? For example, you might tell yourself, "The stock continued to reach new highs and financial pundits thought it was a sound bet." If you have had such thoughts, then you have displayed *cognitive dissonance*, which occurs when newly acquired information conflicts with preexisting understandings, causing discomfort.[28]

When people experience cognitive dissonance, their brain is struggling with two opposite ideas ("I am nice, but I did something that was not nice"), and that struggle is unpleasant. The brain feels uncomfortable with inconsistency. To avoid the feeling, people tend to (1) minimize or change one of the memories, (2) change both memories to match better, or (3) add an additional idea that can attenuate the dissonance.[29]

Racetrack gamblers exemplify how beliefs change to be consistent with past actions. Gamblers just leaving the betting window give the horse they bet on a better chance of winning than people still standing in line to place their bets.[30] That is, before placing the bet, gamblers feel more uncertain than after placing the bet, when their belief changes to be more consistent with their action.

Cognitive dissonance has ramifications in the investment arena. Investors often ignore bad news about a stock they just bought because two ideas—bad news and the fact of the purchase—conflict. Sometimes investors misremember or forget their poor investments. People frequently talk about the investment that doubled or tripled in value, but not the one that lost money. Bad investments challenge their beliefs about being good investors, so they don't want to remember them. Another mental technique that helps to minimize the cognitive dissonance is blame. People look for someone to blame when things go against them. Common investor scapegoats are financial advisors, mutual fund managers, stockbrokers, and portfolio managers.

Investors often are guilty of misremembering their past investment performance.[31] Past performance may not be remembered with perfect accuracy, but if investors are not biased by cognitive dissonance, then their average recall of returns should be close to the actual returns. Because some investors underestimate their performance and others overestimate it, these differences should wash out in the group average. However, the presence of cognitive dissonance leads investors to systematically remember returns as higher than they actually were.

Investors also tend to overestimate their performance relative to the market. Even experienced investors appear to have a similar level of bias. In summary, investors tend to change their memory and beliefs to be more consistent with their positive self-image.

As we mentioned previously, one way to resolve cognitive dissonance is to blame others. Assume that you own a stock or mutual fund that has lost value. You can sell it or hold it. The disposition effect is to hold the loser and ignore the *paper loss*, which is an unrealized capital loss in an investment. This reaction is consistent with the effect of cognitive dissonance. Selling the stock creates more dissonance because it turns a paper loss into an actual loss, which is inconsistent with a positive self-image. However, if you can blame your financial advisor or mutual fund manager for the loss, you can sell the loser stock or mutual fund with less cognitive dissonance. This reaction induces more selling of loser funds, which is the reverse of the disposition effect.

The internal resolutions of cognitive dissonance can negatively affect the financial decision-making process in two ways. First, the filtering of new and negative information that conflicts with investment positions inhibits the effective monitoring of those investments. It also limits the self-evaluation that might improve a person's decision-making process. Second, people may fail to make important decisions or take positive action because contemplating their situation is too uncomfortable. Instead of fixing a problem, they ignore it. For example, they may not sell a stock that has underperformed because doing so would evoke the idea that it was a bad investment, which conflicts with their self-image of being good investors. To overcome cognitive dissonance, you can address the feelings of unease at their source and take appropriate rational action, instead of adapting beliefs or actions to avoid cognitive dissonance.[32]

Do More Investment Experience and Competence Reduce Behavioral Finance Problems?

People can gain greater investment knowledge through education and experience. That education can come from many sources, such as classes, books, blogs, articles, and news reports. This increased financial literacy can lead to better investment decisions. Does more education and financial literacy lead to decisions that are less behaviorally biased?

According to research evidence, investors measuring lower in financial literacy are more prone to the disposition effect. This finding suggests that obtaining more knowledge about investing and behavioral finance helps investors to avoid behavioral biases. Indeed, experienced investors have a lower propensity to suffer from the disposition effect.[33]

People who make many investment mistakes might avoid them by seeking financial advice from qualified advisors. Who seeks financial advice? People with less competence as investors may benefit from advice more than investors with high cognitive ability and experience. But do they seek it? As it turns out, investors with higher investment competence are more likely to seek professional advice and even delegate decisions.[34] Those who are more likely to make investment decisions autonomously have, on average, lower investment competence, are younger and less wealthy, and rely more on price movements and the news media. Unfortunately, the people who are most likely to need financial advice are less likely to seek it.

NOTES

Chapter 1

1 Ellen Langer. 1997. *The Power of Mindful Learning.* New York: Addison-Wesley.

2 Martin Sewell. 2010. "Behavioural Finance." Working paper, University of Cambridge. Available at http://www. behaviouralfinance.net/behavioural-finance.pdf.

3 Robert A. Olsen. 1998. "Behavioral Finance and Its Implications for Stock-Price Volatility." *Financial Analysts Journal* 54:2, 10–18.

4 Brooke Harrington. 2010. "On the Limitations of Behavioral Finance." *Economic Psychology,* October 31. Available at https://thesocietypages.org/economicsociology/2010/10/31/on-the-limitations-of-behavioral-finance/.

5 Herbert A. Simon. 1987. "Bounded Rationality." In John Eatwell, Murray Millgate, and Peter Newman (eds.), *The New Palgrave: A Dictionary of Economics,* 221–225. London: Macmillan.

6 John Authers. 2004. "Why Are Markets Inefficient and What Can Be Done about It?" *Financial Times,* March 9.

7 "Limits to Arbitrage." 2017. InvestorDictionary.com. Available at http://www.investordictionary.com/definition/limits-to-arbitrage.

8 Daniel Kahneman and Amos Tversky. 1979. "Prospect Theory: An Analysis of Decision under Risk." *Econometrica* 47:2, 263–292. Amos Tversky and Daniel Kahneman. 1992. "Advances in Prospect Theory: Cumulative Representation of Uncertainty." *Journal of Risk and Uncertainty* 5:4, 297–323.

9   Morris Altman. 2010. "Prospect Theory and Behavioral Finance."
    In H. Kent Baker and John R. Nofsinger (eds.), *Behavioral
    Finance: Investors, Corporations, and Markets*, 191–209. Hoboken,
    NJ: John Wiley & Sons, Inc.
10 Lucy F. Ackert. "Traditional and Behavioral Finance." In H. Kent
    Baker and Victor Ricciardi (eds.), *Investor Behavior: The Psychology
    of Financial Planning and Investment*, 25–41. Hoboken, NJ: John
    Wiley & Sons, Inc.
11 Morris Altman. 2012. *Behavioral Economics for Dummies*.
    Mississauga, ON: John Wiley & Sons Canada.
12 Hersh Shefrin and Meir Statman. 1985. "The Disposition to
    Sell Winners Too Early and Ride Losers Too Long: Theory and
    Evidence." *Journal of Finance* 40:3, 777–790.
13 Markku Kaustia. 2010. "Disposition Effect." In H. Kent Baker and
    John R. Nofsinger (eds.), *Behavioral Finance: Investors, Corporations,
    and Markets*, 171–189. Hoboken, NJ: John Wiley & Sons, Inc.
14 Nicholas Barberis and Wei Xiong. 2009. "What Drives the
    Disposition Effect? An Analysis of a Long-Standing Preference-
    Based Explanation." *Journal of Finance* 64:2, 751–778.
15 Narasimhan Jegadeesh and Sheridan Titman. 1993. "Returns
    to Buying Winners and Selling Losers: Implications for Stock
    Market Efficiency." *Journal of Finance* 48:1, 65–91. Available at
    http://www.e-m-h.org/JeTi93.pdf. Eugene F. Fama and Kenneth
    R. French. 2012. "Size, Value, and Momentum in International
    Stock Returns." *Journal of Financial Economics* 105:3, 457–472.
16 Sonya Seongyeon Lim. 2006. "Do Investors Integrate Losses
    and Segregate Gains? Mental Accounting and Investor Trading
    Decisions." *Journal of Business* 79:5, 2539–2573.
17 H. Kent Baker and John R. Nofsinger. 2002. "Psychological Biases
    of Investors." *Financial Services Review* 11:2, 97–116.
18 Gerd Gigerenzer, Peter M. Todd, and ABC Research Group. 1999.
    Simple Heuristics That Make Us Smart. New York: Oxford
    University Press.
19 H. Kent Baker and Vesa Puttonen. 2017. *Investment Traps
    Exposed: Navigating Investor Mistakes and Behavioral Biases*. Bingley,
    UK: Emerald Publishing.
20 David Zanoni. 2017. "Momentum Investing Is Supported by
    Academic Research." *Seeking Alpha*, July 25. Available at https://
    seekingalpha.com/article/4090172-momentum-investing-
    supported-academic-research?page=5.

21 Hersh Shefrin. 2000. *Beyond Greed and Fear: Understanding Behavioral Finance and the Psychology of Investing*, 2. Boston, MA: Harvard Business School Press.

22 Amos Tversky and Daniel Kahneman. 1974. "Judgment under Uncertainty: Heuristics and Biases." *Science* 185:4157, 1124–1131. Available at http://psiexp.ss.uci.edu/research/teaching/Tversky_Kahneman_1974.pdf.

23 Daniel Kahneman and Amos Tversky. 1972. "Subjective Probability: A Judgment of Representativeness." *Cognitive Psychology* 3:3, 430–454.

24 Gongmeng Chen, Kenneth A. Kim, John R. Nofsinger, and Oliver M. Rui. 2007. "Trading Performance, Disposition Effect, Overconfidence, Representativeness Bias, and Experience of Emerging Market Investors." *Journal of Behavioral Decision Making* 20:4, 425–451.

25 Kendra Cherry. 2017. "What Is the Availability Heuristic?" *Verywell*, April 27. Available at https://www.verywell.com/availability-heuristic-2794824.

26 Ben Cicchetti. 2015. "Behavioural Finance: The Effect of the Availability Heuristic." *EValue*, November 24. Available at https://www.ev.uk/behavioural-finance-the-effect-of-the-availability-heuristic/.

27 Karolina Lempert. 2015. "What Are Heuristics? Representative vs. Availability Heuristics." *Cambridge Coaching*, May 24. Available at http://blog.cambridgecoaching.com/the-psychology-tutor-what-are-heuristics.

28 Amos Tversky and Daniel Kahneman. 1973. "Availability: A Heuristic for Judging Frequency and Probability." *Cognitive Psychology* 5:2, 207–232.

29 Victor Ricciardi. 2008. "The Psychology of Risk: The Behavioral Finance Perspective." In Frank J. Fabozzi (ed.), *The Handbook of Finance*, volume 3: *Valuation, Financial Modeling, and Quantitative Tools*, 11–38. Hoboken, NJ: John Wiley & Sons, Inc.

30 Albert Phung. 2017. "Behavioral Finance: Key Concepts: Anchoring." *Investopedia*. Available at https://www.investopedia.com/university/behavioral_finance/behavioral4.asp.

31 Kendra Cherry. 2017. "The Affect Heuristic and Decision Making." *VeryWell*, October 16. Available at https://www.verywell.com/what-is-the-affect-heuristic-2795028.

32   Richard Fairchild. 2014. "Emotions in the Financial Markets." In
     H. Kent Baker and Victor Ricciardi (eds.), *Investor Behavior: The
     Psychology of Financial Planning and Investing*, 347–364. Hoboken,
     NJ: John Wiley & Sons, Inc.
33   Melissa L. Finucane, Ali Alhakami, Paul Slovic, and Stephen
     M. Johnson. 2000. "The Affect Heuristic in Judgments of Risks
     and Benefits." *Journal of Behavioral Decision Making* 13:1, 1–17.
34   Baker and Puttonen. 2017.
35   Jason S. Moser, Adrienne Dougherty, Whitney I. Mattson,
     Benjamin Katz, Tim P. Moran, Darwin Guevarra, Holly Shablack,
     Ozlem Ayduk, John Jonides, Marc G. Berman, and Ethan Kross.
     2017. "Third-Person Self-Talk Facilitates Emotion Regulation
     without Engaging Cognitive Control: Converging Evidence
     from ERP and fMRI." *Scientific Reports* 7:1, [4519]. DOI: 10.1038/
     s41598-017-04047-3.
36   Christopher Bergland. 2017. "Silent Third Person Self-Talk
     Facilitates Emotion Regulation." *Psychology Today*, July 28. Available
     at https://www.psychologytoday.com/blog/the-athletes-way/
     201707/silent-third-person-self-talk-facilitates-emotion-regulation.
37   Gerald Hanks. 2017. "Framing Examples in Advertising."
     Available at http://smallbusiness.chron.com/framing-examples-
     advertising-70068.html.
38   Richard J. Taffler and David A. Tuckett. 2010. "Emotional
     Finance: The Role of the Unconscious in Financial Decisions."
     In H. Kent Baker and John R. Nofsinger (eds.), *Behavioral
     Finance: Investors, Corporations, and Markets*, 95–112. Hoboken,
     NJ: John Wiley & Sons, Inc.
39   "Black Monday (1987)." *Wikipedia*. Available at https://
     en.wikipedia.org/wiki/Black_Monday_(1987).
40   Victor Ricciardi. 2017. "The Psychology of Speculation in the
     Financial Markets." In H. Kent Baker, Greg Filbeck, and Victor
     Ricciardi (eds.), *Financial Behavior: Players, Services, Products, and
     Markets*, 481–498. New York: Oxford University Press.
41   Eugene F. Fama. 1998. "Market Efficiency, Long-Term Returns,
     and Behavioral Finance." *Journal of Financial Economics* 49:3,
     283–309.
42   Eugene F. Fama. 1970. "Efficient Capital Markets: A Review of
     Theory and Empirical Work." *Journal of Finance* 25:2, 383–417.
43   Michael Jensen. 1978. "Some Anomalous Evidence Regarding
     Market Efficiency." *Journal of Financial Economics* 6:2–3, 95–101.

44 Harrington. 2010.
45 Colby Wright, Prithviraj Banerjee, and Vaneesha Boney. 2008.
"Behavioral Finance: Are the Disciples Profiting from the
Doctrine?" *Journal of Investing* 17:4, 82–90. Alessandro Santoni
and Arun R. Kelshiker. 2010. "Behavioral Finance: An Analysis
of the Performance of Behavioral Finance Funds." *Journal of Index
Investing* 1:2, 56–72. Nikolaos Philippas. 2014. "Did Behavioral
Mutual Funds Exploit Market Inefficiencies During or After the
Financial Crisis?" *Multinational Finance Journal* 18:1–2, 85–138.
46 Robert J. Shiller. 2003. "From Efficient Markets Theory to
Behavioral Finance." *Journal of Economic Perspectives* 17:1, 83–104.
47 Michael Harris. 2016. "An Explanation of the Persistence
of the Momentum Anomaly." *Seeking Alpha*, February
8. Available at https://seekingalpha.com/article/
3874756-explanation-persistence-momentum-anomaly.

Chapter 2

1 Benjamin Graham. 1973. *The Intelligent Investor*. Revised edition.
New York: HarperCollins.
2 Gus Lubin and Shana Lebowitz. 2015. "58 Cognitive Biases
That Screw Up Everything We Do." *Business Insider*, October 29.
Available at http://www.businessinsider.com/cognitive-biases-
2015-10/#affect-heuristic-1.
3 Bob Bolton. 2015. "Overcoming Investor Biases." Envision
Wealth Planning, August 19. Available at http://
envisionwealthplanning.com/overcoming-investor-biases/.
4 Robert A. Haugen. 2002. *The Inefficient Stock Markets: What Pays
Off and Why*. 2nd ed. Upper Saddle River, NJ: Prentice Hall.
5 Andrei Shleifer. 2000. *Inefficient Markets: An Introduction to
Behavioral Finance*. Oxford: Oxford University Press.
6 Jason Zweig. 2007. *Your Money and Your Brain: How the
New Science of Neuroeconomics Can Help Make You Rich*.
New York: Simon & Schuster.
7 Shahram Heshmat. 2014. "What Is Confirmation Bias?"
Psychology Today, April 23. Available at https://www.
psychologytoday.com/blog/science-choice/201504/
what-is-confirmation-bias.
8 JaeHong Park, Prabhudev Konana, Bin Gu, Alok Kumar,
and Rajagopal Raghunathan. 2010. "Confirmation Bias,
Overconfidence, and Investment Performance: Evidence from

Stock Message Boards." McCombs Research Paper Series No. IROM-07-10, July 12. Available at https://ssrn.com/ abstract=1639470 or http://dx.doi.org/10.2139/ssrn.1639470.

9 Peter Lazaroff. 2016. "How Investors Suffer from Confirmation Bias." *Forbes*, September 28. Available at https://www.forbes. com/sites/peterlazaroff/2016/09/28/confirmation-bias/ #6ef956e94b7d.

10 John Dame and Jeffrey Gedmin. 2013. "Three Tips for Overcoming Your Blind Spots." *Harvard Business Review*, October 2. Available at https://hbr.org/2013/10/ three-tips-for-overcoming-your-blind-spots.

11 Roger Dooley. 2013. "How Warren Buffett Avoids Getting Trapped by Confirmation Bias." *Forbes*, May 7. Available at https://www.forbes.com/sites/rogerdooley/2013/05/07/ buffett-confirmation-bias/#57169ae41616.

12 Keith Hillman. 2016. "Hindsight Bias and Why It's Important to Give Yourself a Break." *Psychology 24*, October 4. Available at http://www.psychology24.org/hindsight-bias-important-give-break/.

13 Kendra Cherry. 2017. "What Is Hindsight Bias?" *Verywell*, March 4. Available at https://www.verywell.com/ what-is-a-hindsight-bias-2795236.

14 Dame and Gedmin. 2013.

15 Neal J. Roese and Kathleen D. Vohs. 2012. "Hindsight Bias." *Perspectives on Psychological Science* 7:5, 411–426.

16 Baruch Fischhoff. 1982. "Debiasing" and "For Those Condemned to Study the Past: Heuristics and Biases in Hindsight." In Daniel Kahneman, Paul Slovic, and Amos Tversky (eds.), *Judgment under Uncertainty: Heuristics and Biases*, 335–351 and 422–444. Cambridge: Cambridge University Press.

17 Mark Griffiths. 2013. "The Beliefs Are Falling: The Illusion of Control in Gambling." DrMarkGriffiths, October 15. Available at https://drmarkgriffiths.wordpress.com/2013/10/15/the-beliefs-are-falling-the-illusion-of-control-in-gambling/.

18 Mark Fenton-O'Creevy, Nigel Nicholson, Emma Soane, and Paul Willman. 2003. "Trading on Illusions: Unrealistic Perceptions of Control and Trading Performance." *Journal of Occupational and Organizational Psychology* 76:1, 53–68.

19 Michael M. Pompian. 2012a. *Behavioral Finance and Wealth Management: How to Build Optimal Portfolios That Account*

for Investor Biases. 2nd ed. Hoboken, NJ: John Wiley
& Sons, Inc.

20 Chana Schoenberger. 2015. "Peter Lynch, 25 Years Later: It's Not
Just 'Invest in What You Know.'" *MarketWatch*, December 28.
Available at http://www.marketwatch.com/story/peter-lynch-
25-years-later-its-not-just-invest-in-what-you-know-2015-12-28.

21 Hisham Foad. 2010. "Familiarity Bias." In H. Kent Baker
and John R. Nofsinger (eds.), *Behavioral Finance: Investors,
Corporations, and Markets*, 277–294. Hoboken, NJ: John Wiley &
Sons, Inc.

22 Victor Ricciardi. 2008. "Risk: Traditional Finance versus
Behavioral Finance." In Frank J. Fabozzi (ed.), *The Handbook of
Finance*, volume 3: *Valuation, Financial Modeling, and Qualitative
Tools*, 11–38. Hoboken, NJ: John Wiley & Sons, Inc.

23 Daniel Kahneman and Amos Tversky. 1979. "Prospect
Theory: An Analysis of Decision under Risk." *Econometrica* 47:2,
263–291.

24 Christopher Milliken, Ehsan Nikbakht, and Andrew C. Spieler.
2017. "Traditional Asset Allocation Securities." In H. Kent
Baker, Greg Filbeck, and Victor Ricciardi (eds.), *Financial
Behavior: Players, Services, Products, and Markets*, 359–377.
New York: Oxford University Press.

25 Harold Evensky. 2017. "Applications of Client Behavior." In
H. Kent Baker, Greg Filbeck, and Victor Ricciardi (eds.), *Financial
Behavior: Players, Services, Products, and Markets*, 523–541.
New York: Oxford University Press.

26 Henrik Cronqvist and Danling Jiang. 2017. "Individual
Investors." In H. Kent Baker, Greg Filbeck, and Victor Ricciardi
(eds.), *Financial Behavior: Players, Services, Products, and Markets*,
45–63. New York: Oxford University Press.

27 Brad Barber and Terrance Odean. 2008. "All That Glitters: The
Effect of Attention and News on the Buying Behavior of
Individual and Institutional Investors." *Review of Financial Studies*
21:2, 785–818. Lily H. Fang, Joel Peress, and Lu Zheng. 2014.
"Does Media Coverage of Stocks Affect Mutual Funds'
Trading and Performance?" *Review of Financial Studies* 27:12,
3441–3466.

28 Victor L. Bernard and Jocob K. Thomas. 1989. "Post-Earnings-
Announcement Drift: Delayed Price Response or Risk
Premium?" *Journal of Accounting Research* 27:3, 1–48.

29 Harrison Hong, Terence Lim, and Jeremy C. Stein. 2000. "Bad News Travels Slowly: Size, Analyst Coverage and the Profitability of Momentum Strategies." *Journal of Finance* 55:1, 265–295.

30 Richard H. Thaler. 1999. "Mental Accounting Matters." *Journal of Behavioral Decision Making* 12:3, 183–206.

31 Drazen Prelec and Duncan Simester. 2001. "Always Leave Home without It: A Further Investigation of the Credit-Card Effect on Willingness to Pay." *Marketing Letters* 12:1, 5–12.

32 Steven Nicholas. 2015. "What Is a Risk Pyramid and Why Is It Important?" *Investopedia*, April 8. Available at http://www.investopedia.com/ask/answers/040915/what-risk-pyramid-and-why-it-important.asp.

33 James J. Choi, David Laibson, and Brigitte C. Madrian. 2009. "Mental Accounting in Portfolio Choice: Evidence from a Flypaper Effect." *American Economic Review* 99:5: 2085–2095.

34 Kapil Jain. 2017. "Never Judge a Decision by Its Outcome: Outcome Bias." *Enrich Wise*, May 6. Available at http://enrichwise.com/2017/05/06/never-judge-a-decision-by-its-outcome-outcome-bias/.

35 Eric J. McNulty. 2015. "Better Lucky Than Smart." Strategy + Business Blogs, June 22. Available at https://www.strategy-business.com/blog/Better-Lucky-than-Smart?gko = 6d3dc.

36 Joseph V. Rizzi. 2014. "Post-crisis Investor Behavior: Experience Matters." In H. Kent Baker and Victor Ricciardi (eds.), *Investor Behavior: The Psychology of Financial Planning and Investing*, 439–455. Hoboken, NJ: John Wiley & Sons, Inc.

37 April Rudin and Catherine McBreen. 2017. "The Psychology of Millennials." In H. Kent Baker, Greg Filbeck, and Victor Ricciardi (eds.), *Financial Behavior: Players, Services, Products, and Markets*, 241–262. New York: Oxford University Press.

38 Victor Ricciardi. 2017. "The Psychology of Speculation in the Financial Markets." In H. Kent Baker, Greg Filbeck, and Victor Ricciardi (eds.), *Financial Behavior: Players, Services, Products, and Markets*, 481–498. New York: Oxford University Press.

39 Michael M. Pompian. 2012b. *Behavioral Finance and Investor Types: Managing Behavior to Make Better Investment Decisions*. Hoboken, NJ: John Wiley & Sons, Inc.

40 Greg B. Davies and Peter Brooks. 2017. "Practical Challenges of Implementing Behavioral Finance." In H. Kent Baker, Greg

Filbeck, and Victor Ricciardi (eds.), *Financial Behavior: Players, Services, Products, and Markets*, 542–560. New York: Oxford University Press.

41   Jason Voss. 2012. "Daniel Kahneman: Psychology for Behavioral Finance." CFA Institute, May 11. Available at https://annual. cfainstitute.org/2012/05/11/psychology-for-behavioral-finance-with-daniel-kahneman/.

42   Bob Seawright. 2013. "Top Ten Ways to Deal with Behavioral Biases." *Above the Market*, January 15. Available at https:// rpseawright.wordpress.com/2013/01/15/top-ten-ways-to-deal-with-behavioral-biases/.

Chapter 3

1   Gary Belsky and Thomas Gilovich. 1999. *Why Smart People Make Big Money Mistakes—and How to Correct Them*. New York: Simon & Schuster.

2   Brad M. Barber and Terrance Odean. 2000. "Trading Is Hazardous to Your Wealth: The Common Stock Investment Performance of Individual Investors." *Journal of Finance* 55:2, 773–806.

3   Brad M. Barber and Terrance Odean. 2001. "Boys Will Be Boys: Gender, Overconfidence, and Common Stock Investment." *Quarterly Journal of Economics* 116:1, 261–292.

4   Brad M. Barber, Yi-Tsung Lee, Yu-Jane Liu, and Terrance Odean. 2014. "The Cross-Section of Speculator Skill: Evidence from Day Trading." *Journal of Financial Markets* 18:C, 1–24.

5   William Samuelson and Richard J. Zeckhauser. 1988. "Status Quo Bias in Decision Making." *Journal of Risk and Uncertainty* 1:1, 7–59.

6   Ziv Carmon and Dan Ariely. 2000. "Focusing on the Forgone: How Value Can Appear So Different to Buyers and Sellers." *Journal of Consumer Research* 27:3, 360–370.

7   Lucy F. Ackert and Richard Deaves. 2010. *Behavioral Finance: Psychology, Decision-Making, and Markets*. Mason, OH: South-Western Cengage Learning.

8   Alex Edmans, Diego Garcia, and Oyvind Norli. 2007. "Sports Sentiment and Stock Returns." *Journal of Finance* 62:4, 1967–1998.

9   Available at https://en.wikipedia.org/wiki/Tulip_mania.

10   Sigmund Freud. 1911. "Formulations Regarding Two Principles of Mental Functioning." In *The Standard Edition of the Complete Psychological Works of Sigmund Freud*. London: Hogarth.

11 Richard Taffler and David Tuckett. 2005. "A Psychoanalytical Interpretation of Dot.com Stock Valuations." Working paper, Social Science Research Network. Available at http://papers.ssrn.com/sol3/papers.cfm?abstract_id = 676635.

12 David Tuckett and Richard Taffler. 2008. "Phantastic Objects and the Financial Market's Sense of Reality: A Psychoanalytical Contribution to the Understanding of Stock Market Instability." *International Journal of Psychoanalysis* 89:2, 389–412.

13 John E. Grable and Michael J. Roszkowski. 2008. "The Influence of Mood on the Willingness to Take Financial Risks." *Journal of Risk Research* 11:7, 905–925.

14 Luigi Guiso, Paola Sapienza, and Luigi Zingales. 2006. "Does Culture Affect Economic Outcomes?" *Journal of Economic Perspectives* 20:2, 23–48.

15 Mark Grinblatt and Matti Keloharju. 2001. "How Distance, Language, and Culture Influence Stockholdings and Trades." *Journal of Finance* 56:3 1053–1073.

16 Alok Kumar, Alexandra Niessen-Ruenzi, and Oliver G. Spalt. 2015. "What's in a Name? Mutual Fund Flows When Managers Have Foreign-Sounding Names." *Review of Financial Studies* 28:8, 2281–2321.

17 Luigi Guiso, Paola Sapienza, and Luigi Zingales. 2009. "Cultural Biases in Economic Exchange?" *Quarterly Journal of Economics* 124:3, 1095–1131.

18 Mark Grinblatt and Matti Keloharju. 2001. "How Distance, Language, and Culture Influence Stockholdings and Trades." *Journal of Finance* 56:3, 1053–1073.

19 Geng Li. 2014. "Information Sharing and Stock Market Participation: Evidence from Extended Families." *Review of Economics and Statistics* 96:1, 151–160.

20 Brad M. Barber and Terrance Odean. 2000. "Too Many Cooks Spoil the Profits: Investment Club Performance." *Financial Analysts Journal* 56:1, 17–25.

21 Brad M. Barber, Chip Heath, and Terrance Odean. 2003. "Good Reasons Sell: Reason-Based Choice among Group and Individual Investors in the Stock Market." *Management Science* 49:12, 1636–1652.

22 George A. Akerlof and Rachel E. Kranton. 2000. "Economics and Identity." *Quarterly Journal of Economics* 115:3, 715–753.

23 Yosef Bonaparte and Alok Kumar. 2013. "Political Activism, Information Costs, and Stock Market Participation." *Journal of Financial Economics* 107:3, 760–786.

24 Markku Kaustia and Sami Torstila. 2011. "Stock Market Aversion? Political Preferences and Stock Market Participation." *Journal of Financial Economics* 100:1, 98–112.

25 Yosef Bonaparte, Alok Kumar, and Jeremy K. Page. 2017. "Political Climate, Optimism, and Investment Decisions." *Journal of Financial Markets* 34:June, 69–94.

26 Robert D. Putnam. 2000. *Bowling Alone: The Collapse and Revival of American Community.* New York: Simon & Schuster.

27 Luigi Guiso, Paola Sapienza, and Luigi Zingales. 2004. "The Role of Social Capital in Financial Development." *American Economic Review* 94:3, 526–556.

28 Luigi Guiso, Paola Sapienza, and Luigi Zingales. 2008. "Trusting the Stock Market." *Journal of Finance* 63:6, 2557–2600.

29 Adnan Balloch, Anamaria Nicolae, and Dennis Philip. 2015. "Stock Market Literacy, Trust, and Participation." *Review of Finance* 19:5, 1925–1963.

30 Robert Olsen. 2012. "Trust: The Underappreciated Investment Risk Attribute." *Journal of Behavioral Finance* 13:4, 308–313.

31 Peter Kelly. 2014. "Dividends and Trust." Working paper, University of Notre Dame. Available at http://ssrn.com/abstract = 2311512.

32 Mariassunta Giannetti and Tracy Yue Wang. 2016. "Corporate Scandals and Household Stock Market Participation." *Journal of Finance* 71:6, 2591–2636.

33 George F. Loewenstein, Elke U. Weber, Christopher K. Hsee, and Ned Welch. 2001. "Risk as Feelings." *Psychological Bulletin* 127:2, 267–286.

34 Camelia M. Kuhnen and Brian Knutson. 2011. "The Influence of Affect on Beliefs, Preferences, and Financial Decisions." *Journal of Financial and Quantitative Analysis* 46:03, 605–626.

35 Alex Edmans, Diego Garcia, and Øyvind Norli. 2007. "Sports Sentiment and Stock Returns." *Journal of Finance* 62:4, 1967–1998.

36 Laura Frieder and Avanidhar Subrahmanyam. 2004. "Nonsecular Regularities in Returns and Volume." *Financial Analysts Journal* 60:4, 29–34.

37 Jędrzej Białkowski, Ahmad Etebari, and Tomasz Piotr Wisniewski. 2012. "Fast Profits: Investor Sentiment and Stock

Returns during Ramadan." *Journal of Banking & Finance* 36:3, 835–845.

38   Mark J. Kamstra, Lisa A. Kramer, and Maurice D. Levi. 2003. "Winter Blues: A SAD Stock Market Cycle." *American Economic Review* 93:1, 324–343.

39   David Hirshleifer and Tyler Shumway. 2003. "Good Day Sunshine: Stock Returns and the Weather." *Journal of Finance* 58:3, 1009–1032.

40   Markku Kaustia and Elias Rantapuska. 2016. "Does Mood Affect Trading Behavior?" *Journal of Financial Markets* 29:C, 1–26.

41   Byoung-Hyoun Hwang. 2011. "Country-Specific Sentiment and Security Prices." *Journal of Financial Economics* 100:2, 382–401.

42   Bradford J. De Long, Andrei Shleifer, Lawrence H. Summers, and Robert J. Waldmann. 1990. "Noise Trader Risk in Financial Market." *Journal of Political Economy* 98:4, 703–738.

43   Yigitcan Karabulut. 2013. "Can Facebook Predict Stock Market Activity?" Working paper, Erasmus University. Available at http://ssrn.com/abstract=1919008.

44   Zhi Da, Joseph Engelberg, and Pengjie Gao. 2014. "The Sum of All FEARS: Investor Sentiment and Asset Prices." *Review of Financial Studies* 28:1, 1–32.

45   Joseph Engelberg and Christopher Parsons. 2016. "Worrying about the Stock Market: Evidence from Hospital Admissions." *Journal of Finance* 71:3, 1227–1250.

Chapter 4

1   Warren Buffett. 2004. "Chairman's Letter." Available at http://www.berkshirehathaway.com/letters/2004ltr.pdf, p. 4.

2   Craig L. Israelsen. 2016. "Comparing the Results of Value and Growth Stock Market Indexes." Fidelity. Available at https://www.fidelity.com/learning-center/trading-investing/trading/value-investing-vs-growth-investing.

3   Kent D. Daniel, David Hirshleifer, and Avanidhar Subrahmanyam. 2001. "Overconfidence, Arbitrage, and Equilibrium Asset Pricing." *Journal of Finance* 56:3, 921–965.

4   Brad M. Barber, Terrance Odean, and Lu Zheng. 2005. "Out of Sight, Out of Mind: The Effects of Expenses on Mutual Fund Flows." *Journal of Business* 78:6, 2095–2120.

5   Brad M. Barber and Terrance Odean. 2008. "All That Glitters: The Effect of Attention and News on the Buying Behavior of

Individual and Institutional Investors." *Review of Financial Studies* 21:2, 785–818.

6 Dong Lou. 2014. "Attracting Investor Attention through Advertising." *Review of Financial Studies* 27:6, 1797–1829.

7 Brad M. Barber and Terrance Odean. 2001. "Boys Will Be Boys: Gender, Overconfidence, and Common Stock Investment." *Quarterly Journal of Economics* 116:1, 261–292.

8 Gary Charness and Uri Gneezy. 2012. "Strong Evidence for Gender Differences in Risk Taking." *Journal of Economic Behavior & Organization* 83:1, 50–58.

9 Mark Grinblatt and Matti Keloharju. 2009. "Sensation Seeking, Overconfidence, and Trading Activity." *Journal of Finance* 64:2, 549–578.

10 Daniel Dorn and Paul Sengmueller. 2009. "Trading as Entertainment?" *Management Science* 55:4, 591–603.

11 Lukasz Markiewicz and Elke U. Weber. 2013. "DOSPERT's Gambling Risk-Taking Propensity Scale Predicts Excessive Stock Trading." *Journal of Behavioral Finance* 14:1, 65–78.

12 Robert R. McCrae. 2009. "The Five-Factor Model of Personality Traits: Consensus and Controversy." In Philip J. Corr and Gerald Matthews (eds.), *The Cambridge Handbook of Personality Psychology*, 148–161. New York: Cambridge University Press.

13 Robert R. McCrae and Paul T. Costa Jr. 1989. "Reinterpreting the Myers-Briggs Type Indicator from the Perspective of the Five-Factor Model of Personality." *Journal of Personality* 57:1, 17–40.

14 Valeria Gazzola, Lisa Aziz-Zadeh, and Christian Keysers. 2006. "Empathy and the Somatotopic Auditory Mirror System in Humans." *Current Biology* 16:18, 1824–1829.

15 Shai Rosenberg, Alan R. Templeton, Paul D. Feigin, Doron Lancet, Jacques S. Beckmann, Sara Selig, Dean H. Hamer, and Karl Skorecki. 2006. "The Association of DNA Sequence Variation at the MAOA Genetic Locus with Quantitative Behavioural Traits in Normal Males." *Human Genetics* 120:4, 447–459.

16 Colin G. DeYoung, Jordan B. Peterson, and Daniel M. Higgins. 2005. "Sources of Openness/Intellect: Cognitive and Neuropsychological Correlates of the Fifth Factor of Personality." *Journal of Personality* 73:4, 825–858.

17 Richard P. Hinz, David D. McCarthy, and John A. Turner. 1997. "Are Women Conservative Investors? Gender Differences in Participant-Directed Pension Investments." In Mitchell

S. Gordon, Olivia S. Mitchell, and Marc M. Twinney (eds.), *Positioning Pensions for the Twenty-First Century*, 91–103. Philadelphia: University of Pennsylvania Press.

18 Vickie Bajtelsmit and Alexandra Bernasek. 1996. "Why Do Women Invest Differently Than Men?" *Financial Counseling and Planning* 7, 1–10.

19 Annika Sunden and Brian Surette. 1998. "Gender Differences in the Allocation of Assets in Retirement Savings Plans." *American Economic Review* 88:2, 207–211.

20 Francine Blau and John Graham. 1990. "Black-White Differences in Wealth and Asset Composition." *Quarterly Journal of Economics* 105:2, 321–339.

21 Erik Hurst, Ming Ching Luoh, and Frank Stafford. 1998. "The Wealth Dynamics of American Families, 1984–94." *Brookings Papers on Economic Activity* 1998:1, 267–337.

22 Ravi Jagannathan and Narayana Kocherlakota. 1996. "Why Should Older People Invest Less in Stocks Than Younger People." *Federal Reserve Bank of Minneapolis Quarterly Review* 20:3, 11–20.

23 Robin K. Chou and Yun-Yi Wang. 2011. "A Test of the Different Implications of the Overconfidence and Disposition Hypotheses." *Journal of Banking and Finance* 35:8, 2037–2046.

24 Lei Feng and Mark S. Seasholes. 2005. "Do Investor Sophistication and Trading Experience Eliminate Behavioral Biases in Financial Markets?" *Review of Finance* 9:3, 305–351.

25 Lei Feng and Mark S. Seasholes. 2005. "Do Investor Sophistication and Trading Experience Eliminate Behavioral Biases in Financial Markets?" *Review of Finance* 9:3, 305–351.

26 Andrea Frazzini. 2006. "The Disposition Effect and Underreaction to News." *Journal of Finance* 61:4, 2017–2046.

27 David Hirshleifer and Tyler Shumway. 2003. "Good Day Sunshine: Stock Returns and the Weather." *Journal of Finance* 58:3, 1009–1032.

28 Brad M. Barber, Chip Heath, and Terrance Odean. 2003. "Good Reasons Sell: Reason-Based Choice among Group and Individual Investors in the Stock Market." *Management Science* 49:12, 1636–1652.

29 Markku Kaustia and Samuli Knüpfer. 2012. "Peer Performance and Stock Market Entry." *Journal of Financial Economics* 104:2, 321–338.

30 Richard W. Sias. 2004. "Institutional Herding." *Review of Financial Studies* 17:1, 165–206.

31 John R. Nofsinger and W. Richard Sias. 1999. "Herding and Feedback Trading by Institutional and Individual Investors." *Journal of Finance* 54:6, 2263–2295.

32 Shlomo Benartzi. 2001. "Excessive Extrapolation and the Allocation of 401 (K) Accounts to Company Stock." *Journal of Finance* 56:5, 1747–1764.

33 Lauren Cohen. 2009. "Loyalty-Based Portfolio Choice." *Review of Financial Studies* 22:3, 1213–1245.

34 Matti Keloharju, Samuli Knüpfer, and Juhani Linnainmaa. 2012. "Do Investors Buy What They Know? Product Market Choices and Investment Decisions." *Review of Financial Studies* 25:10, 2921–2958.

35 Warren Bailey, Alok Kumar, and David Ng. 2011. "Behavioral Biases of Mutual Fund Investors." *Journal of Financial Economics* 102:1, 1–27.

36 Tom Gilovich, Robert Vallone, and Amos Tversky. 1985. "The Hot Hand in Basketball: On the Misperception of Random Sequences." *Cognitive Psychology* 17:3, 295–314.

37 Josef Lakonishok, Andrew Shleifer, and Robert Vishny. 1992. "The Structure and Performance of the Money Management Industry." *Brookings Papers on Economics Activity: Microeconomics*, 339–391.

Chapter 5

1 Amos Tversky and Daniel Kahneman. 1974. "Judgment under Uncertainty: Heuristics and Biases." *Science* 185:4157, 1124–1131.

2 Amos Tversky and Daniel Kahneman. 1981. "The Framing of Decisions and the Psychology of Choice." *Science* 211:4481, 453–458.

3 John R. Nofsinger. 2018. *The Psychology of Investing*. 6th edition. New York: Routledge.

4 Meir Statman, Kenneth L. Fisher, and Deniz Anginer. 2008. "Affect in a Behavioral Asset-Pricing Model." *Financial Analysts Journal* 64:2, 20–29.

5 Hersh Shefrin. 2015. "Investors' Judgments, Asset Pricing Factors and Sentiment." *European Financial Management* 21:2, 205–227.

6 Markus Glaser, Thomas Langer, Jens Reynolds, and Martin Weber. 2007. "Framing Effects in Stock Market Forecasts: The

Difference between Asking for Prices and Asking for Returns."
Review of Finance 11:2, 325–357.

7   Eric J. Johnson and Daniel Goldstein. 2003. "Do Defaults Save
    Lives?" *Science* 302:5649, 1338–1339.

8   Brigitte Madrian and Dennis F. Shea. 2001. "The Power of
    Suggestion: Inertia in 401(k) Participation and Savings Behavior."
    Quarterly Journal of Economics 116:4, 1149–1187.

9   Sheena Sethi-Iyengar, Gur Huberman, and Wei Jiang. 2004. "How
    Much Choice Is Too Much? Contributions to 401(k) Retirement
    Plans." In Olivia Mitchell and Stephen Utkus (eds.), *Pension
    Design and Structure: New Lessons from Behavioral Finance*, 83–95.
    New York: Oxford University Press.

10 Shlomo Benartzi and Richard Thaler. 2002. "How Much Is
    Investor Autonomy Worth?" *Journal of Finance* 57:4, 1593–
    1616.

11 Jeffrey R. Brown, Arie Kapteyn, and Olivia S. Mitchell. 2016.
    "Framing and Claiming: How Information-Framing Affects
    Expected Social Security Claiming Behavior." *Journal of Risk and
    Insurance* 83:1, 139–162.

12 Mauro Guillen and Adrian Tschoegl. 2002. "Banking on
    Gambling: Banks and Lottery-Linked Deposit Accounts."
    Journal of Financial Services Research 21:3, 219–231. Peter Tufano
    and Daniel Schneider. 2009. "Using Financial Innovation to
    Support Savers: From Coercion to Excitement." In Rebecca
    Blank and Michael Barr (eds.), *Insufficient Funds: Savings, Assets,
    Credit, and Banking among Low-Income Households*, 149–190.
    New York: Russell Sage.

13 "Save to Win." Available at https://buildcommonwealth.org/
    work.

14 Peter Tufano. 2008. "Saving Whilst Gambling: An Empirical
    Analysis of UK Premium Bonds." *American Economic Review* 98:2,
    321–326.

15 Felipe Kast, Stephan Meier, and Dina Pomeranz. 2018. "Saving
    More in Groups: Field Experimental Evidence from Chile."
    Journal of Development Economics 133:July, 275–294.

16 Yevgeny Mugerman, Orly Sade, and Moses Shayo. 2014.
    "Long Term Savings Decisions: Financial Reform, Peer Effects
    and Ethnicity." *Journal of Economic Behavior & Organization*
    106:October, 235–253.

17 Edward Cartwright and Amrish Patel. 2013. "How Category Reporting Can Improve Fundraising." *Journal of Economics Behavior & Organization* 87:C, 73–90.

18 Dean Karlan and Margaret A. McConnell. 2014. "Hey Look at Me: The Effect of Giving Circles on Giving." *Journal of Economics Behavior & Organization* 106:C, 402–412.

19 Santosh Anagol and Keith Jacks Gamble. 2013. "Does Presenting Investment Results Asset by Asset Lower Risk Taking?" *Journal of Behavioral Finance* 14:4, 276–300.

20 Uri Gneezy, Arie Kapteyn, and Jan Potters. 2003. "Evaluation Periods and Asset Prices in a Market Experiment." *Journal of Finance* 58:2, 821–837. Charles Bellemare, Michaela Krause, Sabine Kroger, and Chendi Zhang. 2005. "Myopic Loss Aversion: Information Flexibility vs. Investment Flexibility." *Economic Letters* 87:3, 319–324.

21 Maya Shaton. 2017. "The Display of Information and Household Investment Behavior." *Finance and Economics Discussion Series* 2017-043. Washington, DC: Board of Governors of the Federal Reserve System. Available at https://doi.org/10.17016/FEDS.2017.043.

22 Richard H. Thaler and Cass R. Sunstein. 2008. *Nudge: Improving Decisions about Health, Wealth, and Happiness.* New Haven: Yale University Press.

23 Cass R. Sunstein. 2016. "The Council of Psychological Advisers." *Annual Review of Psychology* 67, 713–737.

24 Marianne Bertrand and Adair Morse. 2011. "Information Disclosure, Cognitive Biases, and Payday Borrowing." *Journal of Finance* 66:6, 1865–1893.

25 Sumit Agarwal, John C. Driscoll, Xavier Gabaix, and David Laibson. 2009. "The Age of Reason: Financial Decisions over the Life Cycle and Implications for Regulation." *Brookings Papers on Economic Activity* Fall, 51–117.

26 Victor Stango and Jonathan Zinman. 2009. "Exponential Growth Bias and Household Finance." *Journal of Finance* 64:6, 2807–2849.

27 Oren Bar-Gill. 2009. "The Law, Economics, and Psychology of Subprime Mortgage Contracts." *Cornell Law Review* 94:5, 1073–1151.

28 Yuliya Demyanyk and Otto Van Hemert. 2011. "Understanding the Subprime Mortgage Crisis." *Review of Financial Studies* 24:6, 1848–1880.

29 Richard Thaler and Shlomo Benartzi. 2004. "Save More Tomorrow: Using Behavioral Economics to Increase Employee Savings." *Journal of Political Economy* 112:S1, S164–S187.

30 Greg Engle. 2017. "Moving On: Retiring Danica Patrick Leaving Full-Time NASCAR Cup Seat after Six Seasons." *Autoweek*, 67:23, 22.

31 Shlomo Benartzi, John Beshears, Katherine L. Milkman, Cass R. Sunstein, Richard H. Thaler, Maya Shankar, Will Tucker-Ray, William J. Congdon, and Steven Galing. 2017. "Should Governments Invest More in Nudging?" *Psychological Science* 28:8, 1041–1055.

32 Esther Duflo and Emmanuel Saez. 2003. "The Role of Information and Social Interactions in Retirement Plan Decisions: Evidence from a Randomized Experiment." *Quarterly Journal of Economics* 118:3, 815–842.

33 Esther Duflo, William Gale, Jeffrey Liebman, Peter Orszag, and Emmanuel Saez. 2006. "Saving Incentives for Low- and Middle-Income Families: Evidence from a Field Experiment with H&R Block." *Quarterly Journal of Economics* 121:4, 1311–1346.

34 Duflo, Gale, Liebman, Orszag, and Saez. 2006.

35 Susan M. Dynarski. 2003. "Does Aid Matter? Measuring the Effect of Student Aid on College Attendance and Completion." *American Economic Review* 93:1, 279–288.

36 Bridget Terry Long. 2004. "Does the Format of a Financial Aid Program Matter? The Effect of State In-Kind Tuition Subsidies." *Review of Economics and Statistics* 86:3, 767–782.

37 Eric P. Bettinger, Bridget Terry Long, Philip Oreopoulos, and Lisa Sanbonmatsu. 2012. "The Role of Application Assistance and Information in College Decisions: Results from the H&R Block FAFSA Experiment." *Quarterly Journal of Economics* 127:3, 1205–1242.

38 Hunt Allcott and Todd Rogers. 2014. "The Short-Run and Long-Run Effects of Behavioral Interventions: Experimental Evidence from Energy Conservation." *American Economic Review* 104:10, 3003–3037.

39 Koichiro Ito. 2015. "Asymmetric Incentives in Subsidies: Evidence from a Large-scale Electricity Rebate Program." *American Economic Journal: Economic Policy* 7:3, 209–237.

Chapter 6

1 Carol Loomis. 2012. *Tap Dancing to Work: Warren Buffett on Practically Everything, 1966–2012*, 101. New York: Time Inc.

2   Mark Grinblatt, Matti Keloharju, and Juhani T. Linnainmaa. 2011. "IQ and Stock Market Participation." *Journal of Finance* 66:6, 2121–2164.

3   Dimitris Christelis, Tullio Jappelli, and Mario Padula. 2010. "Cognitive Abilities and Portfolio Choice." *European Economic Review* 54:1, 18–38.

4   Daniel Kahneman. 2001. *Thinking, Fast and Slow*. New York: Farrar, Straus and Giroux.

5   Shane Frederick. 2005. "Cognitive Reflection and Decision Making." *Journal of Economic Perspectives* 19:4, 25–42.

6   Maggie E. Toplak, Richard F. West, and Keith E. Stanovich. 2014. "Assessing Miserly Information Processing: An Expansion of the Cognitive Reflection Test." *Thinking & Reasoning* 20:2, 147–168.

7   Brice Corgnet, Mark DeSantis, and David Porter. 2018. "What Makes a Good Trader? On the Role of Intuition and Reflection on Trader Performance." *Journal of Finance* 73:3, 1113–1137.

8   Eva I. Hoppe and David J. Kusterer. 2011. "Behavioral Biases and Cognitive Reflection." *Economics Letters* 110:2, 97–100.

9   John Nofsinger and Abhishek Varma. 2011. "How Analytical Is Your Financial Advisor?" *Financial Services Review* 16:4, 245–260.

10   Volker Thoma, Elliott White, Asha Panigrahi, Vanessa Strowger, and Irina Anderson. 2015. "Good Thinking or Gut Feeling? Cognitive Reflection and Intuition in Traders, Bankers and Financial Non-experts." *PLoS ONE* 10:4, 1–17.

11   Antoine J. Bruguier, Steven R. Quarz, and Peter Bossaerts. 2010. "Exploring the Nature of 'Trader Intuition.'" *Journal of Finance* 65:5, 1703–1723.

12   Keith Jacks Gamble, Patricia A. Boyle, Lei Yu, and David A. Bennett. 2015. "Aging and Financial Decision Making." *Management Science* 61:11, 2603–2610.

13   Sumit Agarwal, John C. Driscoll, Xavier Gabaix, and David Laibson. 2009. "The Age of Reason: Financial Decisions over the Life Cycle with Implications for Regulation." *Brookings Papers on Economic Activity* 2, 51–117.

14   APCO Insight. 2012. "Senior Financial Exploitation Study." Certified Financial Planner Board of Standards, November. Available at https://www.cfp.net/docs/news-events---supporting-documents/senior-americans-financial-exploitation-survey.pdf?sfvrsn = 0.

15   Patricia A. Boyle, Lei Yu, Robert S. Wilson, Keith Gamble, Aron
     S. Buchman, and David Bennett. 2012. "Poor Decision Making
     Is a Consequence of Cognitive Decline among Older Persons
     without Alzheimer's Disease or Mild Cognitive Impairment."
     PLoS ONE 7:8, 1–5. Keith Jacks Gamble. 2017. "Challenges for
     Financial Decision Making at Older Ages." In Olivia S. Mitchell,
     P. Brett Hammond, and Stephen P. Utkus (eds.), *Financial
     Decision Making and Retirement Security in an Aging World*, 33–45.
     Oxford: Oxford University Press.

16   Eric Bonsang and Thomas Dohmen. 2015. "Risk Attitude and
     Cognitive Aging." *Journal of Economic Behavior & Organization*
     112:C, 112–126.

17   George M. Korniotis and Alok Kumar. 2011. "Do Older Investors
     Make Better Investment Decisions?" *Review of Economics and
     Statistics* 93:1, 244–265.

18   Tibor Besedeš, Cary Deck, Sudipta Sarangi, and Mikhael Shor.
     2012. "Age Effects and Heuristics in Decision Making." *Review of
     Economics and Statistics* 94:2, 580–595.

19   Merrill M. Mitler, Mary A. Carskadon, Charles A. Czeisler,
     William C. Dement, David F. Dinges, and R. Cutris Graeber. 1988.
     "Catastrophes, Sleep, and Public Policy: Consensus Report."
     Sleep 11:1, 100–109.

20   Yiannis Kountouris and Kyriaki Remoundou. 2014. "About
     Time: Daylight Saving Time Transition and Individual Well-
     Being." *Economics Letters* 122:1, 100–103.

21   Yvonne Harrison. 2013. "The Impact of Daylight Saving Time
     on Sleep and Related Behaviours." *Sleep Medicine Reviews* 17:4,
     285–292.

22   William D. S. Killgore. 2010. "Effects of Sleep Deprivation on
     Cognition." In Gerard A. Kerkhof and Hans Van Dongen (eds.),
     Progress in Brain Research 185, 105–129. Amsterdam: Elsevier.

23   Hui-Chu Shu. 2010. "Investor Mood and Financial Markets."
     Journal of Economic Behavior & Organization 76:2, 267–282.

24   Mark J. Kamstra, Lisa A. Kramer, and Maurice D. Levi. 2000.
     "Losing Sleep at the Market: The Daylight Saving Anomaly."
     American Economic Review 90:4, 1005–1011. Russell Gregory-Allen,
     Ben Jacobsen, and Wessel Marquering. 2010. "The Daylight
     Saving Time Anomaly in Stock Returns: Fact or Fiction?" *Journal
     of Financial Research* 33:4, 403–427.

25 Ian Garrett, Mark J. Kamstra, and Lisa A. Kramer. 2005. "Winter Blues and Time Variation in the Price of Risk." *Journal of Empirical Finance* 12:2, 291–316.

26 William D. S. Killgore, Thomas J. Balkin, and Nancy J. Wesensten. 2006. "Impaired Decision Making Following 49 h of Sleep Deprivation." *Journal of Sleep Research* 15:1, 7–13. William D. S. Killgore, Erica L. Lipizzi, Gary H. Kamimori, and Thomas J. Balkin. 2007. "Caffeine Effects on Risky Decision Making after 75 Hours of Sleep Deprivation." *Aviation, Space, and Environmental Medicine* 78:10, 957–962. William D. S. Killgore. 2007. "Effects of Sleep Deprivation and Morningness-Eveningness Traits on Risk-Taking." *Psychological Reports* 100:2, 613–626. William D. S. Killgore, Nancy L. Grugle, Desiree B. Killgore, Brian P. Leavitt, George I. Watlington, Shanelle McNair, and Thomas J. Balkin. 2008. "Restoration of Risk-Propensity during Sleep Deprivation: Caffeine, Dextroamphetamine, and Modafinil." *Aviation, Space, and Environmental Medicine* 79:9, 867–874. Benjamin S. Mckenna, David L. Dickinson, Henry J. Orff, and Sean P. A. Drummond. 2007. "The Effects of One Night of Sleep Deprivation on Known-Risk and Ambiguous-Risk Decisions." *Journal of Sleep Research* 16:3, 245–252.

27 William D. S. Killgore, Nancy L. Grugle, and Thomas L. Balkin. 2012. "Gambling When Sleep Deprived: Don't Bet on Stimulants." *Chronobiology International* 29:1, 43–54.

28 Michael Pompian. 2012a. *Behavioral Finance and Wealth Management: How to Build Optimal Portfolios That Account for Investor Biases*. 2nd edition. Hoboken, NJ: John Wiley & Sons, Inc.

29 Alexander Klos, Elke Weber, and Martin Weber. 2005. "Investment Decisions and Time Horizon: Risk Perception and Risk Behavior in Repeated Gambles." *Management Science* 51:12, 1777–1790.

30 George A. Akerlof and William T. Dickens. 1982. "The Economic Consequences of Cognitive Dissonance." *American Economic Review* 72:3, 307–319.

31 William Goetzmann and Nadav Peles. 1997. "Cognitive Dissonance and Mutual Fund Investors." *Journal of Financial Research* 20:2, 145–158.

32 Pompian. 2012a, 81.

33 Newton Da Costa Jr., Marco Goulart, Cesar Cupertino, Jurandir Macedo Jr., and Sergio da Silva. 2013. "The Disposition Effect and Investor Experience." *Journal of Banking & Finance* 37:5, 1669–1675.

34 Kremena Bachmann and Thorsten Hens. 2015. "Investment Competence and Advice Seeking." *Journal of Behavioral and Experimental Finance* 6:C, 27–41.

INDEX